Building
Stereo
Speakers

Building Stereo Speakers

Plans ▪ Parts Tools ▪ Techniques

Andy Wells

McGraw-Hill Book Company

New York St. Louis San Francisco Auckland Bogotá
Guatemala Hamburg Johannesburg Lisbon London Madrid
Mexico Montreal New Delhi Panama Paris San Juan
São Paulo Singapore Sydney Tokyo Toronto

BUILDING STEREO SPEAKERS

A **VTX** book.

1 2 3 4 5 6 7 8 9 SEM SEM 8 7 6 5 4 3

ISBN 0-07-069251-3

LIBRARY OF CONGRESS CATALOGING IN PUBLICATION DATA

Wells, Andy J.
  Building stereo speakers.

  Includes index.
  1. Loud-speakers—Design and construction—Amateurs' manuals. I. Title.
TK9968.W47   1983   621.389′334   82-20340
ISBN 0-07-069251-3

Contents

Introduction

Each year thousands of stereo speaker systems are built in school shops, home basements, garages, kitchens, and other working areas. With a few tools and some basic skills, you can assemble the wood and electronic parts to make a successful speaker. Imagine the pride of turning up the volume and listening to the enjoyable sound of your own handbuilt system. You will probably find that you have saved a few dollars, too.

Of course, almost any project will turn out better if you have a few helpful tips. This speaker building guide has many project suggestions to help you with choosing a project and selecting parts through building and testing the speakers. Many drawings and photographs are included to show important and interesting details. Step-by-step procedures are explained to help you with each part of construction. The information is based on many years of research and hundreds of successful homebuilt speaker projects. Simple plans are included for the first-time builder. Experienced builders may want to add changes to the plans or follow the suggestions for creating their own speaker designs.

As you begin, take time to study this building guide and select your materials wisely. Use patience on the small details and build the speaker carefully. Your efforts will be well rewarded by the many compliments you receive and the personal satisfaction of knowing "you built it yourself"!

CHAPTER ONE

Starting Your Speaker Project

Welcome to speaker building! The most interesting part of your whole stereo system will probably be your speakers. They change the electrical signals into sound, producing enjoyable music; and you can build them yourself!

In this chapter, you will learn about the role of stereo speakers and the function of each speaker part as well as differences in speaker size, power, and sound quality. Important information is explained and several "Builder's Decision" questions are asked. By considering each question, you can determine which speaker plan or design would be best for your needs. After making your project decisions, you may want to custom design your own speakers using the design information at the end of this chapter.

1.1
The Role of Stereo Speakers

Listening to good music from a good stereo system is an enjoyable experience. The music should sound clear, be as loud as

Fig. 1-1 A stereo system which has separate components.
(Mitsubishi Audio Systems.)

you like it, and seem as though the musicians are performing right in front of you. Stereo systems may be small and compact, or larger with separate components as shown in Fig. 1-1.

The System

Each stereo system can be considered as three separate sections: sound sources, amplifiers, and speakers, as shown in Fig. 1-2.

The sound sources produce small electrical signals from the recorded music and include tape decks, turntables (record players), AM-FM receivers, and microphones. Since most sound sources are stereo, they actually produce two separate music signals. The signals represent approximately the left and right sides of the performers during recording and playing of the

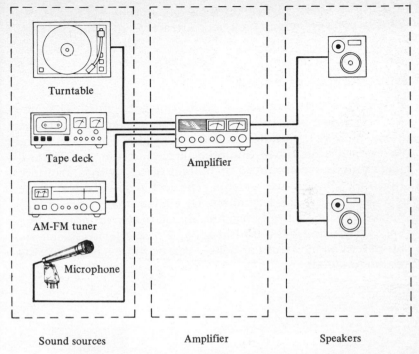

Fig. 1-2 The three main sections of a stereo system.

music. The left and right sides are often called *channels* when discussing stereo equipment.

The amplifier is considered to be the "heart" of a stereo system. It increases the power (energy) of the music signals and contains the controls for the sound such as volume, tone, and several switches. The amplifier is connected directly to each speaker and its power must be considered when selecting a speaker project.

The speakers are often the largest part of most stereo systems. They are placed several feet apart and in front of the listening area where they change the amplified music signals into enjoyable sound. Speakers greatly affect the way a stereo system sounds; and they can be easily built at home, school, or other work areas. Figure 1-3 shows an example of five sizes of speaker projects which look very attractive and sound great!

Three Ranges of Sound

Stereo speakers produce a wide range of musical sounds (*pitches*) which are often described in three general terms: *bass* (low), *midrange* (middle), and *treble* (high). The bass sounds represent drums, tubas, and other large instruments. The midrange sounds are produced by human voices, banjos, trumpets, and other similar instruments. The treble sounds are created by violins, flutes, and cymbals, Of course, many instruments, such as a piano, actually produce music in two or more of these ranges. By using bass, midrange, and treble terms, discussion of different sounds from a speaker can be more easily described and understood.

Fig. 1-3   Examples of five speaker units.

Differences in Sound

Although most types of stereo speakers operate in a similar way, they often sound slightly different, much like the voices of good singers. Differences in speaker sound are due to size, power, quality of parts, and cabinet design. The sound of a speaker is often described with casual words such as: boomy, tight, dynamic, bright, or full. Unfortunately, these words have different meanings for each person. Speaker performance can be more accurately described with three technical terms: *loudness*, *frequency response*, and *distortion*. Loudness is measured in decibel (dB) units by using a small handheld *sound level meter*. The frequency response is the range of sound being produced from the lowest to highest pitches and is measured in units called *hertz* (Hz). Distortion is any noise or changes in the sound which are not part of the music. These three terms are often used in discussing stereo sound performance. You will soon find them very helpful in selecting, building, and testing your speaker project.

1.2
Basic Parts of a Speaker

Some small stereo speakers are simple and have only a few parts as shown in Fig. 1-4. The speaker in Fig. 1-5 is larger, has many parts, and is capable of high performance. This speaker is called "three-way" because it has separate drivers for the bass, midrange, and treble sounds. However, to produce high-quality sound in any speaker, all parts must be carefully selected and assembled to work together as a system.

Drivers

The *driver* is the most important part of any speaker because it converts the electrical signals to actual sound. Figure 1-6 shows a driver and its main assemblies: the *cone*, the *frame*, and the *magnet*.

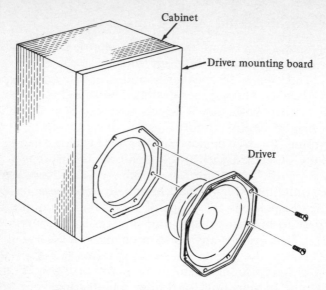

Cabinet

Driver mounting board

Driver

Fig. 1-4 A small low-powered speaker.

Some small speakers use just one driver designed to cover a wide part of the musical range. This type of driver is often called a *"full-range"* driver. Although it does not reproduce the very low and very high frequencies, it does produce good overall sound considering its smaller size and low cost. A speaker with a full-range driver will often be the easiest to build and may be a good choice for a beginner.

Many speakers have two, three, or more drivers of different sizes as shown in Fig. 1-7. Each driver produces a range of sounds related to the driver's size. For example, large drivers (called *woofers*) produce bass sounds; and small drivers (called *tweeters*) produce treble sounds. Combining these two drivers (two-way system) allows the speaker to produce a wider range of music than just a single driver. A third driver of medium size (called a midrange) is often added between the woofer and tweeter. The three drivers (three-way system) allow the speaker to cover the full range of musical sounds.

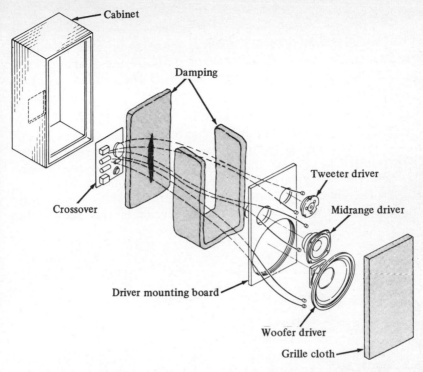

Fig. 1-5 A high-performance speaker which has many parts.

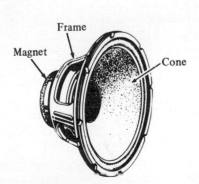

Fig. 1-6 The three main assemblies of a driver.

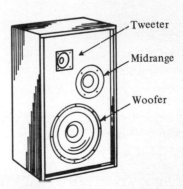

Fig. 1-7 A high-performance, three-way speaker using three drivers.

Cabinet

The speaker cabinet (enclosure) is made from many pieces as shown in Fig. 1-8. It must be strongly built and also attractive since it is a part of your room furniture. The cabinet has three important functions:

1. *To Physically Support the Drivers.* The front of the cabinet is called the "driver mounting board." It must be very sturdy to prevent vibration and noise when the driver is producing sound. The driver mounting board supports the drivers which face forward at the correct spacing and position.
2. *To Prevent Sound Cancellation.* Figure 1-9 shows how sound can travel from the back of the driver to the front of the

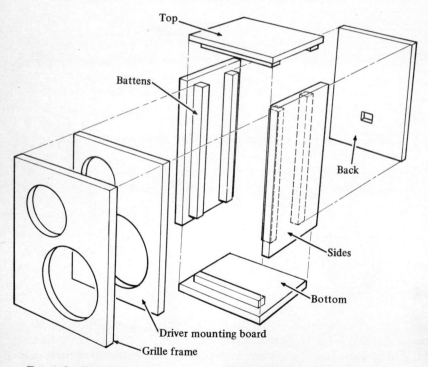

Fig. 1-8 Wood pieces which are used to make a completed speaker cabinet.

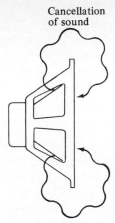

Cancellation
of sound

Fig. 1-9 An example of sound movement which causes cancellation when no cabinet is used.

driver and cancel the front sound if nothing blocks the path. A driver without a cabinet will have poor low bass sound. For example, automotive stereo systems are sometimes incorrectly installed because the speaker drivers are placed in the back window area without the use of cabinets. As a result, most of the low bass sound is lost. However, if the drivers were mounted in small, simple boxes, the overall quality of sound would be greatly improved.

3. *To Load the Woofer Driver.* A speaker cabinet contains air which the woofer cone must move back and forth very quickly while producing sound. The air acts as a *"load"* for the driver cone because the cone must push the air with each movement. The air load helps reduce any extra cone movement after the music signals have changed or stopped, and thus helps prevent unnatural ("mushy" or "muddy") speaker sounds.

The inside design of the cabinet greatly affects sound performance. *Acoustic suspension, ported reflex,* and *passive radiator* are the names of three common designs for cabinets which are used in home stereo systems. The performance of each design is slightly different.

Acoustic Suspension. This style is sometimes called the sealed box or infinite *baffle* speaker. Simple box construction is used, as shown in Fig. 1-10. The sealed air pressure inside the cabinet allows good sound performance when creating loud music. The low bass response is quick, clean, and natural sounding. This is an excellent design for beginners due to its simple design and easy construction.

Ported Reflex. This design will often use a slightly larger cabinet with a special tube (called a tuning duct) or port as shown in Fig. 1-11. The port allows the sound inside the cabinet to project outward to improve low bass sound. However, exact cabinet and port sizes are important for top performance, especially when creating very loud sounds. Since size and construction are critical, this design may be a good challenge for the advanced builder.

Passive Radiator. The woofer in the passive radiator design is called *"passive"* because it has no electrical parts and is driven by the air pressure produced by another regular woofer as shown in Fig. 1-12. This design has good low bass performance and a very natural sound. However, the passive woofer and the driving woofer must be carefully selected to work as a team. The cabinet must often be made larger to hold both woofers.

Damping Material

Sound is reflected back onto the woofer driver by hard wall surfaces inside the cabinet. If there is too much reflected sound, the music will seem boomy and unnatural. To reduce this problem, sound absorbing (*damping*) material is added inside the cabinet on the bottom, back, and sides. Glass fiber insulation or polyester batting are good sound damping materials which help control reflected sound. Damping material is not usually placed on the top or front of the cabinet since it may work loose and fall onto the woofer driver.

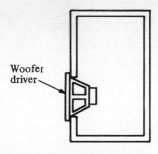

Fig. 1-10 An inside view of an acoustic suspension speaker which has a sealed cabinet.

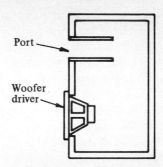

Fig. 1-11 An inside view of a ported speaker which uses a tuning duct.

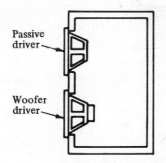

Fig. 1-12 An inside view of a passive radiator speaker which has two drivers.

Grille Cloth

The grille is a part that has nothing to do with producing sound but is used on most speakers. *Grille cloth* is usually a thin material which lets the sound pass through, protects the drivers from dirt, and improves the speaker's appearance. Actually, speakers would sound a little better without the grille cloth, but most people like the looks of a cloth cover. A strong grille cloth could protect your drivers from damage, especially if little children are playing near the speakers. Grille cloths should be removable to allow inspection of the drivers.

Crossovers

Crossovers improve sound performance and help prevent *burn-out* of the small tweeters when using loud music. A crossover is a simple electronic circuit of coils, capacitors, and terminals used in speakers with two or more drivers for better power-handling ability and performance. With a crossover, each driver receives only the music signals it can reproduce. A two-way crossover separates the sound into low and high ranges. A three-way crossover, as shown in Fig. 1-13, adds a middle range and is used with woofer, midrange, and tweeter drivers.

Level Controls

Level controls (often called *L-pads*) are small adjustable devices installed in the electronic circuit of the speaker to control driver loudness. Many better-quality speakers have level controls. They are usually fastened on the back of the speaker or on the driver mounting panel, as shown in Fig. 1-14. Level controls can be used to adjust the loudness of the midrange or tweeter drivers to suit personal *listening taste*. Their low cost makes them a good investment when building your own two- or three-way system.

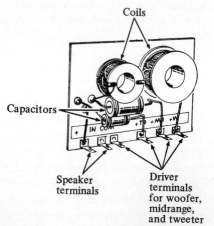

Fig. 1-13   A three-way crossover circuit.

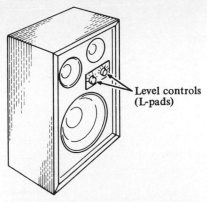

Level controls
(L-pads)

Fig. 1-14 L-pad speaker controls
are used to adjust sound loudness.

1.3
Determining Speaker Power

One of the first items to consider when planning your project
is *speaker power*. Speaker power is actually a common term
which refers to both sound power [measured in *decibel* (dB)
units of loudness] and electrical power [measured in *watts* (W)].
To find the right speaker power for you, consider the sound
loudness you expect to hear, the size of the listening room, and
the power of your amplifier.

Sound Loudness

Do you like your music loud so you can feel it, or soft and re-
laxing? The loudness desired for music is important in selecting your speaker power.

Loudness of speakers can be measured in dB units with a
meter such as the one shown in Fig. 1-15. The softest sound
your ears can hear would be 1 dB, and the loudest would be
about 130 dB which is the beginning of pain. A loudness chart
of some common sounds is shown in Fig. 1-16. Notice that an
average speaking voice is about 63 dB.

Fig. 1-15 A low-cost sound meter which measures sound loudness (dB). (*Radio Shack Division, Tandy Corp.*)

Some people think loud music (about 90 dB or more) is just for young people or nightclub dancing. However, classical music of a live symphony orchestra will produce up to 100 dB or more of sound for the audience in front. If you enjoy classical music and play it soft, you may miss part of the true sound.

In general, if you like loud music, you will want a stereo system which can produce 90 to 110 dB of sound. If you prefer softer music, you will need only 70 to 80 dB of sound at your listening location.

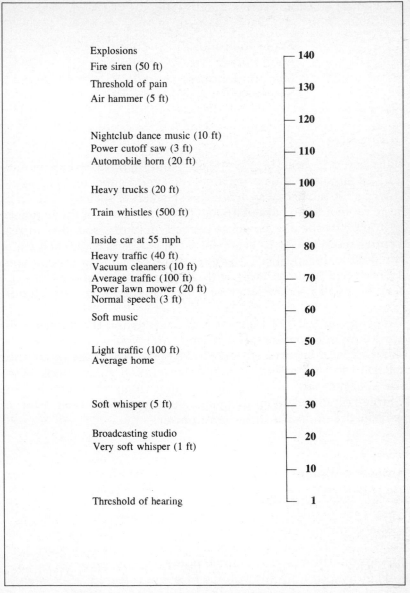

Fig. 1-16 Common sounds and their dB levels.

Builder's Decision. How much sound do you want at the listening location?

Super loud music	110 dB
Loud music	100 dB
Medium loudness	90 dB
Soft music	80 dB

Room Size

Have you ever been near a speaker, and then walked away and noticed how the music became weaker? Sound quickly loses power as it moves away from the speaker. If speakers are in a large room and far [about 16 feet (ft) or more] from the listener, a little extra speaker power is needed. Actually, sound requires 4 times more power to keep the same loudness level each time you double the speaker to listener distance. For example, if you hear a certain music level with 20 W at 8 ft, as shown in Fig. 1-17, you will need 80 W at 16 ft to hear the same sound loudness.

As you can see, the bigger the room size and the farther you are from your speakers, the more power you will need. When choosing your speaker size, try to keep the size of the room and speakers in proportion. If you have a small room, bookshelf-size speakers will produce good sound. However, if you are in a large recreation room or gymnasium, you should use a large speaker design and a little more power.

Amplifier Power

Of all the technical data about stereo systems, amplifier power creates the greatest interest. "How much power does it have?" is the common question. Answers such as "20 watts," "50 watts," or "120 watts" are often given. However, a more important question is "How much power do you need?"

When you turn up the volume of a low-powered, 15-W stereo system, the sound becomes loud (about 105 dB). However, if you were to compare that sound to the loudness of a high-pow-

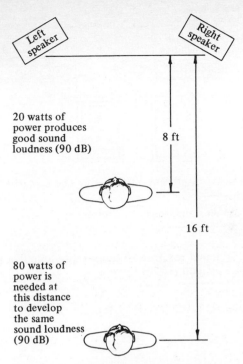

20 watts of power produces good sound loudness (90 dB)

8 ft

16 ft

80 watts of power is needed at this distance to develop the same sound loudness (90 dB)

Fig. 1-17 Moving twice as far from a speaker requires 4 times more power to keep the same sound level.

ered 150-W system as shown in Fig. 1-18, you would discover the sound has become only twice as loud. In other words, increasing the amplifier power by 10 times made the sound only 2 times (10 dB) louder.

The chart in Fig. 1-19 compares typical sound loudness expected when using different amplifier power. As can be seen from the chart, high-powered amplifiers are often needed for areas where very loud (115-dB) music is desired.

When comparing speaker loudness, you will find some sound slightly louder than others even though the amplifier power to both is the same. This difference in speaker loudness occurs because only a part of the amplifier's power is converted to

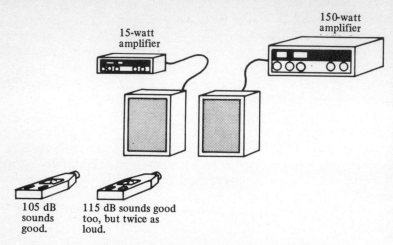

105 dB sounds good.

115 dB sounds good too, but twice as loud.

Fig. 1-18 A sound requires 10 times more amplifier power to appear twice as loud (10-dB increase).

Description	Sound loudness (dB) near the speaker	Amplifier power (W rms)
Strong voice-speaking	75	0.015
Soft music	85	0.15
Moderately loud	95	1.5
Loud music	105	15
Very loud music	115	150
Extremely loud music	125	1500
Threshold of pain	130	——

Fig. 1-19 A chart comparing the typical loudness expected from amplifiers of different power ratings.

sound. Most of the power becomes heat, which is wasted. The amount of sound developed is determined by the speaker's *efficiency*. Descriptions of speaker designs and speaker parts often refer to the efficiency as being high, medium, or low. You can generally expect high-efficiency speaker designs to produce slightly more loudness than low-efficiency designs.

When planning your speaker project, you will need to consider the output power of your amplifier so you can select parts to match your amplifier's power. Amplifier power is measured in watts *rms* (*root-m*ean-*s*quare) per channel. The power rating per channel is usually advertised, labeled on the back of the amplifier, or mentioned in the service or instruction manual. If there is no power rating, the amplifier may likely be a low-powered, 10 to 20 W rms per channel amplifier.

Your speakers and amplifier must have similar power ratings to work together as a system. If your amplifier has more power than your speakers (for example: 40 W rms amplifier, 20 W rms speakers), you may burn out the drivers with loud sound. For best results, design your speakers so they will have a power rating equal to or slightly larger than the amplifier output. However, there is one condition you must always avoid with any speaker to prevent damage! Do *not* turn the volume control of any amplifier so far up that the sound (which will be very loud) becomes distorted and unnatural. At this high volume, the amplifier has reached its power limit and is producing high-frequency distortions which quickly burn out the tweeter drivers. Even a small, 20-W rms amplifier will burn out the tweeter of a large 40-W rms speaker under this distorted sound condition. Once again, the two most important ways to prevent speaker damage are:

1. Select electronic parts and a speaker design with a power rating equal to or larger than the amplifier.
2. Keep the volume of *any* amplifier below the level where it begins to sound distorted. In other words, if you turn up your music and it begins to have a sharp, raspy, or fuzzy sound, quickly turn it back down or you may damage your speakers.

Builder's Decision. What is the output power rating of your amplifier in watts rms per channel?

1.4
Understanding Sound Quality

The main reason for using a stereo system is to hear all of the *natural sound* in your music. This means that your speakers must produce the very low-, medium-, and high-frequency sounds of music without any noticeable distortion.

Speakers usually affect sound quality more than any other stereo component. As you select drivers and other parts for building your speakers, be sure to look and work for good sound quality by considering these two important items: frequency response and sound distortion.

Frequency Response

Sound is really just the movement (vibration) of air which we can hear. Our frequency range (response) of hearing is about 18 Hz to 20,000 Hz when we are young. As we grow older, however, our hearing is gradually reduced, so by the age of 50 many people will hear only about one-half the frequency range that a young person hears. Do not worry about it, however, because a good stereo system is still *very* enjoyable, even at 50.

The frequency response of drivers or speakers is often shown by a graph such as the one shown in Fig. 1-20. Notice the dark, wavy line on the graph. This line indicates the response (sound loudness) at various test frequencies. Although the input signal is constant, the output response varies. When the response (loudness of the sound) has dropped to one-half (−3 dB) of its average full level, the driver has reached its *cutoff frequency*. In the example of Fig. 1-20, the average response is 80 dB. The cutoff point is 77 dB (80 dB − 3 dB). This 77-dB point is reached at 100 Hz and 9000 Hz. Therefore, the range of usable frequency response is 100 Hz to 9000 Hz. By knowing the range

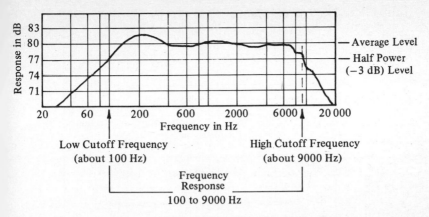

Fig. 1-20 A speaker graph showing the low and high cutoff frequencies which are 3 dB below the average signal level.

of frequency response, you can determine what portion of the full frequency range of music is being reproduced by that driver or speaker.

Although frequency range is important, the *"flatness"* of the performance graph is also important. Figure 1-21 compares the frequency performance of two speakers. Notice that both graphs have the same cutoff points, but the strength of the sound changes in system A by almost 3 dB above or below the average test level of 86 dB. System B has less than 1 dB of sound change from its average sound level, which produces a flat curve and better sound performance. Remember, any change in sound of 1 dB or more can be heard, so speakers should be designed to produce as flat a frequency as possible.

Stereo frequency response should cover the full range of hearing and music. However, it is very difficult and expensive to build a speaker to cover this wide range. A more practical frequency range for your speakers can be determined by considering the music source and your music taste. Frequency ranges of common music sources are given in the following list for your use:

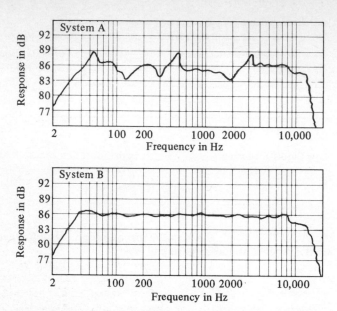

Fig. 1-21 A comparison of two speaker graphs. System B has better performance than system A because of the flatter response curve with less than 1 dB of change from the average level.

AM radio	50–10,000 Hz
FM radio	50–15,000 Hz
Cassette deck (lower quality)	about 50–12,000 Hz
Cassette deck (higher quality)	about 32–18,000 Hz
Turntable (or record player)	about 32–20,000 Hz

When selecting a speaker design or parts, keep the music source in mind. A speaker designed for AM radio, for example, does not need the high-frequency response that would be necessary for a turntable music source.

Your music taste should also be considered. If you enjoy a lot of low bass and high treble sounds in your music, you will need a wide frequency response from the speaker. Many young people enjoy strong, low-frequency music, especially when dancing. Strong, low frequencies below 100 Hz can actually be felt on your body. If you would like to hear these strong, low frequencies from your speakers, use a high-power 10-, 12-, or 15-in woofer driver.

Builder's Decision.   When considering music source and music taste, what frequency range will you need for your speakers?

Distortions of Sound

Have you listened to music from a speaker and noticed buzzing sounds, fuzzy music, or rasping noises? As you listen to your favorite music, does your hearing seem to grow tired (a condition called *"listening fatigue"*)? These are just a few of the sound quality problems caused by distortion in a speaker. Of course, every component of a stereo system (including the music source, amplifier, and speakers) adds a little distortion to the music. Even the very best stereo equipment has some distortion, but it will not be noticed or a problem if it is less than 1 percent of the music.

When building your speakers, distortions can be kept very low by using high-quality parts and good construction. The three main types of speaker distortion are: *noise*, *clipping*, and *transient*. When these distortions of a speaker are low, you feel like you can listen to and enjoy music for many hours.

Noise.   This is static, rattling, rasping, hissing, or other strange sounds. It can be caused by loose joints, cracked boards, loose fasteners, poor electrical connections, damaged drivers, objects touching the speaker, or objects touching the drivers. An example of a common noise is the rattle caused by small objects which have fallen through the grille of a dash-mounted car speaker. A tear or crack in the paper cone of a driver as shown in Fig. 1-22 may also cause a buzzing noise in the music.

Cracked cone

Fig. 1-22 A torn driver cone which causes a distorted noise.

Clipping.   Physical or electrical clipping causes a harsh sound in your music as you turn the volume up to high levels. It is most noticeable at the lower bass frequencies which use most of the speaker power. It is caused by either of two conditions:

1. Physical clipping results when the speaker drivers are forced to the limits of their movement.
2. Electrical clipping occurs when an amplifier reaches the limit of its power and the sound signal is chopped or clipped off.

Clipping is very harmful to your speakers and may cause damage or burnout of the drivers. The best way to avoid clipping is to match the speaker to the amplifier power and use *less* than full sound power.

◈ **A WORD OF CAUTION:**   An amplifier can reach its full power even though the volume control is less than its full range setting. This can happen if the bass tone control is turned up, the loudness control is *on*, or a tape deck music source is turned to full output level. The position of the volume control cannot be used to determine the power being delivered to the speakers.

Transient. This term refers to the time delay of the speaker driver cones as they respond to a music signal. This type of distortion is somewhat like a truck entering a highway. Because of its heavy load, the truck requires time to gain speed or slow down and stop. Driver cones, especially woofers, also need time to start moving and then stop again. Of course, they must do this many times each second. Any slight delay in their movement is called *transient distortion*. You may not notice this distortion right away; but when a speaker has good transient response with low distortion, music will sound more natural. For example, reproduced piano music will sound more realistic; and chimes, drums, and cymbals will sound like chimes, drums, and cymbals. You cannot do much to reduce transient distortion except to buy higher-quality drivers which, presumably, are better engineered for less distortion.

1.5
Planning Your Speaker Project

Speaker projects such as those shown in Fig. 1-23 have been designed to be attractive, sound good, and meet the needs of

Fig. 1-23 Examples of completed speaker projects.

the builder. You may have already decided what type and size of speaker you intend to build. However, if you are not sure what speaker project would be best for you, use the project questions, typical performance data, and suggestions in this section to help you plan your project.

Speaker Project Questions

As you select your speaker project, consider the five following questions:

1. How loud do you enjoy your music?
2. How large is the listening room?
3. What amplifier output power in watts rms per channel will be used?
4. What frequency response would you like?
5. What price range can you afford?

The answers to these questions will help determine the type of speaker that best meets your needs.

Typical Performance Data

The chart in Fig. 1-24 lists the typical performance you might expect from each speaker size as well as suggested drivers and crossovers for estimating building cost. Compare your answers from the five previous project questions to the information on the chart. The comparisons should help you determine which speaker size would be best for your project.

Project Suggestions

The following suggestions apply to building two speakers (a matched pair) for stereo sound.

1. *Develop Project Ideas.* Inspect factory-built speakers at a stereo equipment or consumer electronics showroom. No-

SPEAKER SIZE (IDENTIFIED BY WOOFER DIAMETER)

Item	5-in speaker	8-in speaker	10-in speaker	12-in speaker	15-in speaker
Maximum expected sound loudness 6 ft from the speaker, dB	Moderate 96	Strong 105	Loud 110	Very loud 112	Super loud 115
Room size, ft^2	50–100	80–190	110–240	140–300	180–480
Amplifier power, W rms/channel	5–20	10–35	15–60	20–100	30–150
Frequency response, Hz	110–14,000	80–15,000	60–18,000	42–19,000	30–20,000
Type and number of drivers for comparing cost	1 5-in full-range	1 8-in full-range (or) 1 8-in woofer 1 4-in tweeter 1 two-way crossover	1 10-in woofer 1 4-in tweeter 1 two-way crossover (or) 1 10-in woofer 1 5-in midrange 1 3-in tweeter 1 three-way crossover	1 12-in woofer 1 5-in midrange 1 3-in tweeter 1 L-pad 1 three-way crossover	1 15-in woofer 1 6-in midrange 2 3-in tweeters 2 L-pads 1 three-way crossover

Fig. 1-24 A comparison of typical specifications and parts for five speaker sizes. Exact performance will vary depending on cabinet size, design, and parts used.

tice the overall dimensions, the number of drivers in the cabinet, and the general appearance of the speaker. Check the performance data and listen to the sound. When you find a speaker you would really like to build, make a rough sketch of the unit. Add dimensions to the sketches and jot down general notes about materials and construction. These will be helpful in choosing or designing your speaker project.

2. *Use a Speaker Plan.* Whether you choose a prepared speaker plan from Chap. 2 or design your own, a project plan (even if it is just sketches) will save you time and material.

3. *Use Acoustic Suspension Design.* The acoustic suspension (sealed cabinet) speaker is the simplest to design and easiest to build. Very few, if any, cabinet adjustments are required after building to provide good sound performance.

4. *Use Identical Parts on Both Speakers.* When buying parts, select parts of the same size, style, model, and type for both speakers so they will look and sound alike.

5. *Work Carefully.* Take time to do your best work on each part of speaker designing and building. Careful planning, work, and craftsmanship with tools are important for good speaker appearance, performance, and your safety.

1.6
Designing the Speaker Cabinet

The use of prepared speaker plans for building cabinets is a helpful aid to many beginning builders. Five different sets of complete plans for popular speaker sizes are included in Chap. 2 for your reference. However, if you enjoy a more challenging project, you may want to design your own speaker cabinet and plans.

Most speakers are designed to meet the needs of hundreds of other people, and many compromises must be made which you may not like. One advantage you have is that the speaker you design will be for your needs. It can be designed to be the right size for your building material, fit your listening area (you may want it a certain size to fit a special location), and produce the sound performance you like.

Speaker designing is somewhat of a cross between science, art, and user conditions. The science is the formulas, tables, and charts. The art is the dimensions, selection of materials, and construction which make a speaker look good. The user conditions are the listening room size, surfaces, amplifier power, and speaker placement. These three items affect *all* speakers in terms of sound and appearance.

As you begin designing speaker cabinets, your first few designs should be for the acoustic suspension (sealed-box) system. An acoustic suspension speaker, compared to ported or other designs, has simple construction and tends to forgive small mistakes in cabinet size. You probably have a basic cabinet size or woofer driver diameter in mind for your design. Your first step, then, is to match the cabinet size and woofer driver by considering speaker cabinet volume.

Speaker Cabinet Volume

The air volume inside the speaker cabinet helps improve low-frequency response of the woofer driver. The size of the cabinet volume depends on the woofer's cone edge (*suspension*), cone size, stiffness of movement (*compliance*), and other specifications. Fortunately, most drivers of the same diameter have similar specifications. Therefore, based on driver diameter, a range of cabinet volumes can be recommended for each woofer size. These recommended cabinet volumes have been determined by engineering measurements and the practical experience of many speaker manufacturers and builders.

The chart in Fig. 1-25 suggests inside cabinet volumes for average drivers based on their diameter. To use the chart, find your woofer driver size, then read directly down to the suggested range of cabinet volumes listed in cubic feet (ft^3). All of the area below the woofer drawing represents the range of recommended cabinet volumes. For example, the chart shows that most 12-in woofer drivers will work well with a cabinet volume anywhere between 1.7 and 3.5 ft^3. When designing your cabinet, select a cabinet size which has a volume within the recommended range. In general, cabinets smaller than the rec-

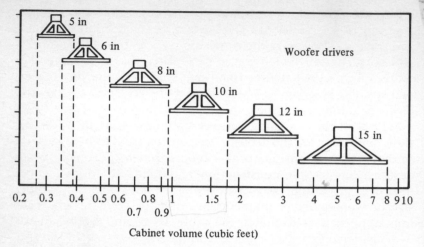

Fig. 1-25 Chart showing suggested range of speaker cabinet volumes which work well for most woofer drivers.

ommended range of volume often sound weak at low frequencies. On the other hand, cabinets larger than the recommended volume may sound mushy and will not handle as much amplifier power.

Speaker Cabinet Shape and Size

Once you have found the suggested internal cabinet volume for your woofer from the chart in Fig. 1-25, you are ready to convert this volume to internal cabinet dimensions. Audio engineers have found that a depth, width, and height ratio of 0.6 to 1 to 1.6 will produce good speaker performance. Not surprisingly, this is similar to the *Golden Ratio* of dimensions used by artists and designers since the days of the Egyptian pyramids. This ratio produces a cabinet design that will look good and sound more natural because of its relatively flat low-frequency response.

An example of using the suggested cabinet dimensions ratio follows: If you have a 15-in woofer and desire to make a speaker cabinet 20 in wide, multiply the width by 0.6 to determine the depth (20 in × 0.6 = 12 in) and then multiply the width by 1.6 to determine the height (20 in × 1.6 = 32 in) which gives the final depth, width, and height dimensions of 12 in by 20 in by 32 in. You can convert these dimensions to volume by multiplying them together (12 in × 20 in × 32 in = 7680 in³). The volume in cubic inches can be changed to cubic feet by dividing by 1728 (7680 in/1728 = 4.44 ft³). When you refer back to the chart in Fig. 1-25, the 4.44 ft³ are well within the range (3.4 to 8 ft³) for the 15-in woofer. Therefore, your choice of cabinet size should produce good speaker performance.

The chart in Fig. 1-26 can also be used to find the depth, width, and height for your cabinet design. To use the chart, find the desired cabinet volume (in cubic feet) on the bottom of the chart. Follow this volume number line up the chart to each of the three curved lines. At the intersection of each line, read to the left or right to find the depth, width, and height dimensions.

Another method which also works is to read just the width from the chart, then multiply the width by the Golden Ratio (as described previously) to get the depth and height. These numbers can be rounded off to one decimal place for easier use.

In some cases, when building speakers, you may prefer to use different cabinet sizes than the suggested ratio. For example, your boards may not be quite wide enough or you may not be able to fit the cabinet in a certain location. Slight changes (less than 10 percent) usually do not noticeably affect performance. The 12 in by 20 in by 32 in design mentioned earlier, for example, can be changed to 13 in by 21 in by 30 in to fit under a wall shelf.

All measurements discussed so far have been for the *inside* of the cabinet. You will have to consider material thickness and type of corner joints being used to find the outside cabinet dimensions. The volume chart has been designed to take the volume of the drivers, crossover, L-pad, and glass fiber damping into consideration. You do *not* need to adjust your cabinet volume for these items when using the volume chart.

Rectangular boxes have been suggested as speaker cabinets but a wedge or pyramid shape may also work very well if you

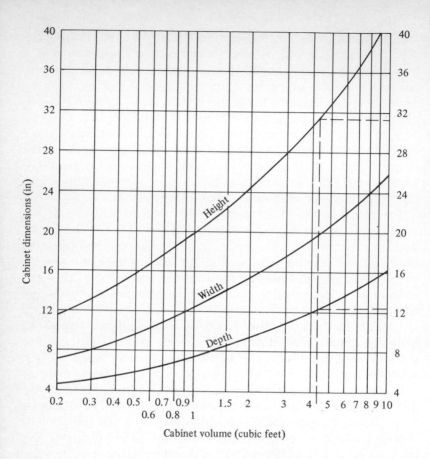

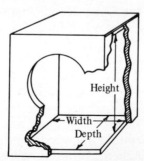

Fig. 1-26 A chart to find the inside cabinet depth, width, and height from a selected volume.

keep the recommended inside volume. These shapes are more difficult to build but are useful for rear car window placement or other special areas.

Driver Placement

In general, the woofer should be near the bottom so the low-frequency sounds can be projected outward by the floor. Also, the woofer is the heaviest' part and makes the speaker more stable. The tweeter should·be close to ear level height since high frequencies project outward with only a small angle of dispersion (spread). The midrange should be between the woofer and tweeter in a vertical pattern as shown in Fig. 1-27. If size does not allow this, place the drivers on an angle, but do not put them side-by-side. When drivers are side-by-side, their projected sound waves may cancel in some areas which will give the listening room "dead" spots of reduced sound. Try to place the drivers on the mounting board so there is at least ½ in of space between their mounting flanges. This space helps provide cabinet strength and good performance at crossover frequencies. If the drivers are mounted off-center, make the second

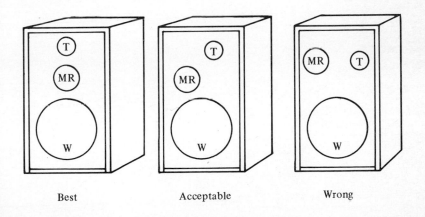

Fig. 1-27 Placement of drivers for best performance.

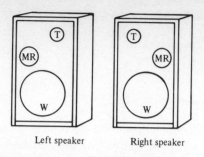

Left speaker   Right speaker

Fig. 1-28   Arrangement of drivers when building two speakers for stereo sound.

speaker a mirror image of the first as shown in Fig. 1-28. This allows you to place the speakers so both will have the tweeter drivers on the inward side for better balance and performance.

CHAPTER TWO

Selecting Speaker Materials, Tools, and Plans

A large variety of materials are available for building your speakers and many can be purchased from local suppliers. Wood, screws, nails, and glue, for example, can be found at most lumber yards or hardware stores. Electronic parts (drivers, crossovers, L-pads, etc.) can be purchased at electronic supply stores or through mail-order catalogs. Many suppliers often stock the same parts, so shopping for the best price could save you money. As you select parts for your project, try to match each part to the total speaker system in terms of desired appearance and performance.

Common tools typically found in home workshops are used for building speakers. Choose tools which are in good condition and the right size for the project. Many helpful suggestions and brief technical explanations for selecting materials and tools are included in this chapter.

At the end of the chapter, five different sets of building plans are also included for your use. Each speaker plan offers different features and information on typical performance, building materials, parts layout, and construction. The plans can be a helpful guide if you are a beginner, or a useful reference if you are designing your own speaker project.

This chapter begins with choosing the speaker drivers. By purchasing the drivers and other electronic parts first, you can check exact sizes, such as driver diameters, before marking or cutting mounting holes. Also, if your parts are mail-ordered, you can work on assembling the cabinet while the parts are being shipped.

2.1
Choosing the Drivers

The large assortment of drivers available, as shown in Fig. 2-1, makes driver selection interesting. Most drivers are called *"dynamic"* because they use a cone attached to a moving coil of wire near a magnet to produce sound from electrical signals. The main parts of a common dynamic driver are shown in Fig. 2-2.

Four popular categories are used to describe drivers: woofer, midrange, tweeter, and full-range. A woofer, as shown in Fig. 2-3, is the largest and often the most expensive driver. It must be able to absorb all of the amplifier's output power without being damaged or creating distortions to their low-frequency sound.

The midrange driver is smaller in size for reproducing the middle frequencies of music and voice. It should be enclosed and sealed on the back side as shown in Fig. 2-4. An enclosed driver will not be affected by sound produced inside the cabinet by the woofer.

The tweeter is the smallest driver in size and performs well at the very high frequencies. A common cone tweeter is shown in Fig. 2-5.

A full-range driver is often used where just one driver will be installed in a speaker. It is designed to have a wide frequency response which will produce acceptable sound over most of the music frequency range. Full-range drivers are often used on small or low-cost systems.

Fig. 2-1   An assortment of common speaker drivers.

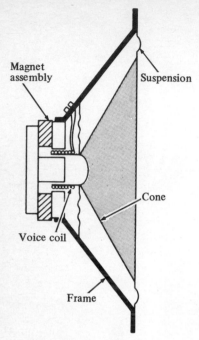

Magnet assembly

Suspension

Cone

Voice coil

Frame

Fig. 2-2 A dynamic driver showing the main parts.

Woofer Driver

12-in diameter
Rated: 60 W rms, 120 W peak
54-oz ceramic magnet
2½-in voice-coil diameter
8-ohms impedance
Free air resonance: 28 Hz
Frequency response: 40–6000 Hz
Aluminum voice coil
Polyfoam cone edge

Fig. 2-3 A woofer driver with typical specifications.

Midrange Driver

5-in diameter
Rated: 30 W rms
        50 W peak
10-oz magnet
1-in aluminum voice coil
Frequency response: 390–6200 Hz

Fig. 2-4 A sealed midrange driver with typical specifications.

Fig. 2-5 An example of a cone tweeter.

The specifications of a driver's performance are often listed by the manufacturer. Each specification will be explained in this section; and specific information about woofers, mid-ranges, and tweeters will be presented. By comparing specifications, you can select the best drivers for your speaker project.

Driver Diameter

Diameter is the most common driver specification and is determined by measuring across the driver front to the outside edge of the *mounting flanges* as shown in Fig. 2-6. Frequency response is greatly affected by driver diameter. Small drivers have small cones which can move very quickly and thus produce high frequencies. Large drivers have large (and heavy) cones which move slower to produce good low-frequency response. Although a driver has an advertised diameter (12 in, for ex-

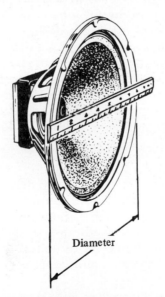

Diameter

Fig. 2-6 Driver diameter is measured from the outer edges of the mounting flanges.

ample), it may actually measure slightly more or less (12¼ in). Therefore, when building your speakers, be sure to check the exact size of the driver diameter and its mounting flanges before laying out and cutting the mounting hole.

Woofer Diameter.   Diameters of 5, 6, 8, 10, 12, and 15 in are typical for woofer drivers. In general, as a driver diameter becomes larger, it can absorb more amplifier power, produce louder sound, and have a better low-frequency response. However, there is a practical limit (about 15 in) to woofer diameter for most speakers. As the diameter of woofers increases, the cabinet size, transient distortion, and driver cost also increase.

Keep your speaker project in mind as you select the woofer diameter. The small woofers (5-, 6-, and 8-in) are useful for compact or bookshelf-size speakers. The medium-size woofers (10- and 12-in) are popular because the notes from some instruments, especially pianos, seem to sound natural and full. The large (15-in) woofers are useful where good low-frequency response and/or very loud music are desired.

If you are using automotive speaker drivers which are oval in shape, you can make comparisons to round drivers by using the average size of the oval driver. To find the average driver size, add the smallest and largest oval diameters and then divide by two. For example, a 6-in by 9-in speaker has an average size of 7½ in, and should have similar performance to an 8-in round woofer.

Midrange Diameter.   Most midrange drivers have diameters of about 4, 5, or 6 in. Select a midrange diameter which can easily be placed in the available mounting area on the driver mounting board. For most medium-size speakers (10- and 12-in woofers) midrange diameters of about 4 or 5 in work well. The 15-in woofer speakers should have midrange diameters of 5 or 6 in.

Tweeter Diameter.   Diameters of 2, 3, or 4 in are common for tweeters. However, outside tweeter diameter has very little effect on performance. Consider tweeter diameter in terms of available area for placement on the driver mounting board.

Power Rating

Many drivers, like amplifiers, are rated in watts rms; but a few are listed in terms of *"music power"* or *"peak power."* Music power can vary depending on the music being used. If music power or peak power are listed for a driver, reduce them by at least 50 percent when comparing them to amplifier power. As an example, 60 W music power (or peak power) is about equal to 30 W rms power (60 W music × 0.50 = 30 W rms).

All power ratings for drivers and speakers must be greatly reduced if you are using test tones. The steady frequency of test tones can quickly build up heat in a driver and cause damage. When using a steady test signal, keep the amplifier power very low (less than $1/10$ of the driver or speaker power rating).

Musical instrument speaker drivers differ from stereo speaker drivers in their power-handling ability. Therefore, regular stereo speaker drivers should *not* be used for amplifying systems with musical instruments such as guitars. Guitars, for example, can produce a steady note which lasts for several seconds and is similar to a test tone. Such notes can burn out a regular woofer driver even at half power.

Woofer Power. The power rating of the woofer driver should be slightly larger than the amplifier power.

Midrange Power. Power ratings on most midrange drivers will be much less than the woofer. Most midrange drivers will *not* handle more than about 25 W rms because of their small voice coils. Fortunately, less amplifier power is needed to produce good midrange sound. In general, many builders look for a midrange power rating which is about half of the woofer power. To be on the safe side, select midrange drivers with a little extra power rating.

Tweeter Power.   You should select a tweeter with a power rating equal to the midrange power (about half of the woofer power). If you cannot find a tweeter with a large enough power rating, use two tweeters and connect them electrically for twice as much power-handling ability.

Voice Coils

The *voice coil* inside the driver consists of many turns of fine wire wrapped and glued onto a *bobbin* (short tube) as shown in Fig. 2-7. The power of the amplifier is used by the voice coil to create an electromagnetic force which reacts with the permanent magnet of the driver. This reaction causes the voice coil and bobbin to move. The bobbin is connected to the cone,

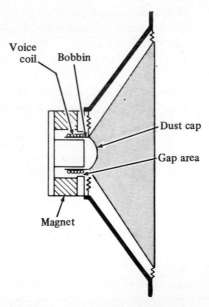

Fig. 2-7   Cutaway view showing
voice coil, bobbin, and dust cap.

so any movement of the voice coil and bobbin is transferred to the cone where it becomes sound.

The diameter of the voice coil affects the power-handling ability and frequency response of the driver. Voice coil diameter is often listed in the driver's specifications, but if it is not known, you can sometimes see the diameter by turning the driver sideways and looking through the large metal frame holes. Larger voice coils have larger wire and more bobbin surface area for better cooling and, therefore, can handle more power. However, smaller voice coils move more quickly and are necessary for good high-frequency response.

In better-quality drivers, the voice coil wire is held on the bobbins with high-temperature epoxy glue. Also, the bobbins are made from aluminum to improve cooling and power rating.

A small *dust cap* is attached to the front of the driver cone to cover the bobbin. This cover helps keep dirt or dust out. Using a driver *without* a cabinet will also allow dirt to enter from the back side of the driver. Dirt or dust between the voice coil and magnet (*gap area*) may cause a rubbing noise during use.

Woofer Voice Coils.   The voice coil diameter on small woofers should be at least 1½ in. Larger woofers of 10-, 12-, or 15-in diameter should have a voice coil diameter of at least 2 or 2½ in to reduce the chance of the voice coil overheating and burning out.

Midrange Voice Coils.   Most midrange voice coils will be about 1 to 1½ in in diameter.

Tweeter Voice Coils.   Tweeters must have very light and small voice coils of about 1-in diameter to produce good high-frequency response. To improve cooling and power ratings, some models have a special liquid sealed inside the voice coil area.

Magnet Size

Speaker drivers use permanent magnets to create magnetic fields around the voice coil area. Driver magnets are most often compared by their weight. As the weight becomes larger, the driver efficiency will usually become better and, therefore, sound louder. There is a practical limit for each driver design, however, as increasing the magnet weight (or size) further would have very little effect on performance. Most drivers use *ceramic magnets*, but a few use the more powerful *Alnico magnets* (which are about twice as strong for their weight). For comparison, a 20-ounce (oz) ceramic magnet will be about equal in strength to a 10-oz Alnico magnet.

◈ **A WORD OF CAUTION:**   To make an advertisement look better, some manufacturers list the weight of the *magnet assembly*. However, the magnet assembly includes several heavy iron pieces. Do *not* compare the weight of a magnet assembly to the weight of a magnet.

Woofer Magnets.   A woofer requires the largest magnet because during low frequencies its voice coil must move large distances (up to 1 in or more in some drivers). A larger magnet can provide a large and strong magnetic area through which the voice coil can react. The following table suggests common ceramic magnetic weights for better-quality woofer drivers:

Diameter	Magnet Weight
8 in	20 oz or more
10 in	24 oz or more
12 in	30 oz or more
15 in	32 oz or more

Midrange Magnets.   Midrange drivers require smaller magnets than the woofers because voice coil movement is less. Ceramic magnet weights of 10 oz or more will produce efficient performance from most midrange drivers.

Tweeter Magnets. Magnetic weights of 4 to 10 oz are common for dynamic tweeters.

Speaker Cones

Driver Cones. The driver cone produces sound by moving the air in front of it. The cone is connected to and moved by the voice coil bobbin. The cone must be strong, yet light in weight to move quickly for natural-sounding music. The color of the cone is usually black so it will not show under the grille cloth. A few drivers have white cones which perform equally as well as the black cones.

A small cone is sometimes installed on the front of a large cone, especially on 8-in full-range drivers. The small cone is called a *"whizzer"* cone as shown in Fig. 2-8. Whizzer cones help produce higher frequencies for better performance when using only one driver.

Woofer Cones. Woofer cones are usually made from a special high-quality fiber material to withstand the forces during high power. With strong low frequencies, for example, the cone is quickly forced to move and it must be very rigid to prevent bending or tearing. Exact cone material is not usually specified for woofers.

Fig. 2-8 A driver with a whizzer cone for high frequencies.

Midrange Cones.   Most midrange drivers use cones, but a few use a plastic dome as shown in Fig. 2-9. Because of its dome shape, the driver can often spread the sound better (better *dispersion*) throughout the front area of the speaker.

Tweeter Cones.   Tweeters which use the small, light cone as shown in Fig. 2-10a are usually the least expensive. These small drivers have good high-frequency response although power ratings may be less than 20 W rms.

Tweeters without Cones

Although cone tweeters are common, several other types of tweeters without cones can be used for good high-frequency performance. Each type of tweeter has certain features to consider.

Dome Tweeters.   In this type of driver, a rounded dome of very thin plastic (often *Mylar*) is used in place of a cone as shown in Fig. 2-10b. The curved dome shape produces very good sound dispersion. The frequency response will typically be 2000 to 20,000 Hz. The power ratings of dome tweeters usually run high and may be up to 50 W.

Piezo Tweeters.   These tweeters, as shown in Fig. 2-10c, are becoming very popular in speaker systems. No voice coils or magnets are used. Instead, a small, but special, ceramic crystal (*piezoelectric*) is used which bends when an electrical signal is applied. The crystal is placed in a horn-shaped frame which efficiently projects and disperses the sound outward. The small piezoelectric crystal has very good frequency response which may typically be 2000 to 24,000 Hz or more. These tweeters are usually low-priced since they have so few parts. The power ratings may run from 10 to 20 W rms, depending on the model.

Fig. 2-9 A dome
midrange driver.

(a) Cone tweeter

(b) Dome tweeter

(c) Piezo tweeter

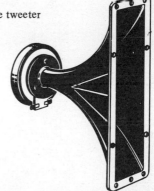

(d) Horn tweeter

Fig. 2-10 Examples showing four types of tweeters.

Horn Tweeters. A horn tweeter, as shown in Fig. 2-10d, may be either dynamic or piezoelectric. The horn is used in place of a cone or dome and helps spread the sound for good dispersion. Horns often produce very natural-sounding cymbal and brass instrument music.

Suspension

The suspension (soft cone edge) holds the cone in alignment and allows it to move in or out to produce sound. Suspensions (sometimes called *"surrounds"*) must be flexible and airtight. The stiffness of the suspension affects the efficiency of the driver and its ability to damp cone movement once the signal has stopped.

Woofer Suspension. The woofer's low-frequency performance is noticeably affected by the type of suspension used. The folded-paper suspensions as shown in Fig. 2-11 are usually stiffer and are a good choice for ported or reflex speakers where damping of cone movement is important at low frequencies.

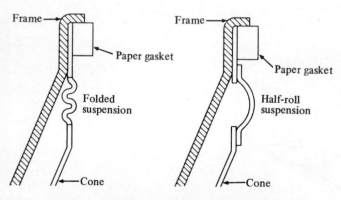

Fig. 2-11 An example of a folded fabric and a half-roll suspension.

The *half-roll suspensions* which are polyfoam or butyl rubber are often used in acoustic suspension speakers. Experience has shown that butyl rubber is slightly better than polyfoam for low-frequency performance.

Compliance is a measure of the energy needed to move the cone. Half-roll suspensions allow the cone to move easily and are often called high-compliance drivers. High-compliance drivers are an excellent choice for acoustic suspension speakers if the cabinets are within or near the suggested volume.

Midrange and Tweeter Suspension. The suspension is smaller for the cones of midrange and tweeter drivers because of less cone movement. Information and specifications for these drivers often are not listed.

Frequency Response

The frequency response of a driver will give you some idea of its performance and can be helpful when comparing drivers or selecting frequencies. As described earlier in Chap. 1, frequency response is measured by determining the low and high frequencies where the sound drops 3 dB in loudness. This 3-dB loudness drop means at that frequency the driver is producing only half of its full power.

Graphs, when available, are more useful in describing frequency response than just numbers since variations of performance within the frequency response range can be seen. In general, flatter response graphs indicate more natural-sounding driver performance.

Woofer Frequency Response. Graphs usually are not given for woofers because their frequency response depends on their cabinet. As an example, a driver can be advertised with a 35- to 2200-Hz frequency response. However, if a cabinet is too small, the frequency response of this same driver may be increased to about 55 to 2400 Hz. The flatness of the response will also change with the design and size of each cabinet.

Free-air resonance is sometimes listed along with frequency response. It refers to the easiest frequency the driver can produce when it is *out* of a cabinet using a constant signal power. The free-air resonance value is useful in comparing the low-frequency performance of two or more drivers. For example, a driver with a free-air resonance of 24 Hz will probably sound slightly stronger at low frequencies than a driver with a free-air resonance of 40 Hz. Drivers with very low free-air resonance frequencies are a good choice for acoustic suspension speakers, especially if the cabinets are near the smaller sizes of suggested cabinet volume.

Midrange Frequency Response. Frequency response for midrange drivers should reach from about 600 Hz to at least 6000 Hz. The response should also be flat and have less than ± 3 dB of signal level change. The flatness of the response is important since our hearing ability is very sensitive in this range and even small sound loudness changes can be heard. Figure 2-12 shows a graph of a midrange response. The graph shows that the response is usable from about 700 Hz to 10,000 Hz.

Tweeter Frequency Response. Your music source and taste in music should be considered when selecting the tweeter. Most tweeters have a response of at least 2000 to 18,000 Hz. However, many go much higher and may produce good performance up to 20,000 Hz, 22,000 Hz, or even 24,000 Hz. Most people cannot hear above 20,000 Hz, but the effect of high frequencies (harmonics) over 20,000 Hz from musical instruments can be heard as they react with the lower frequencies. Some musical experts say this reaction between high frequencies is important for a speaker to produce natural-sounding music.

If a graph of tweeter response is available, such as the one shown in Fig. 2-13, notice the flatness of the response line. Several peaks or dips of over ±3 dB may indicate poor performance. Drivers which show the flattest response usually have the most natural sound.

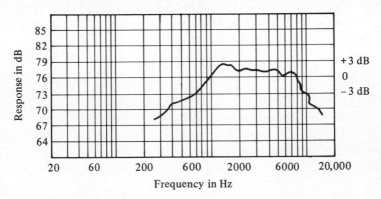

Fig. 2-12   Graph of a midrange frequency response.

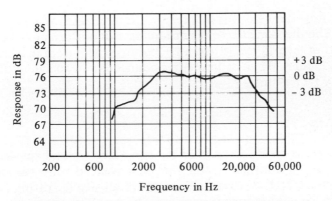

Fig. 2-13   Graph of tweeter response showing relatively smooth (about ± 1 dB) performance at the higher frequencies.

Driver Impedance

The *impedance* of a driver describes how it will draw electrical power from the amplifier. Most drivers have an 8-ohm impedance which is the standard impedance necessary to allow an amplifier to deliver its full rated power. If the impedance gets too low (below 2 ohms) the amplifier will usually shut down because the driver is drawing too much power. If the impedance is too high (above 32 ohms), too little power is being used and the driver will sound weak. Drivers of 4-, 8-, or 16-ohms impedance can be used, but 8-ohms impedance is standard and will usually produce the best results.

If driver impedance is not known, you can measure the voice coil resistance with an ohmmeter and determine the impedance. The resistance should be about 75 percent of the impedance rating. Typical resistance and impedance of common drivers are as follows:

> 3-ohms resistance = 4-ohms impedance
> 6-ohms resistance = 8-ohms impedance
> 12-ohms resistance = 16-ohms impedance

The impedance of the woofer, midrange, and tweeter drivers should be the same for uniform loudness. If one driver is 4 ohms, for example, and the others are 8 ohms, the 4-ohm driver may sound louder. When a driver impedance is not specified, it will usually be 8 ohms.

Sensitivity

Sensitivity is a dB rating used for some drivers and speakers to determine how much sound can be produced from the power being used. Not all drivers have their sensitivity rating listed, but it is becoming more common. The sensitivity measurement is usually made with a sound level meter at a distance of 1 meter (m) (3.3 ft). The measurement is made directly in front of the driver using 1 W rms [2.83 volts (V) rms] of power as shown in Fig. 2-14. Different test frequencies are used, depending on the size of the driver.

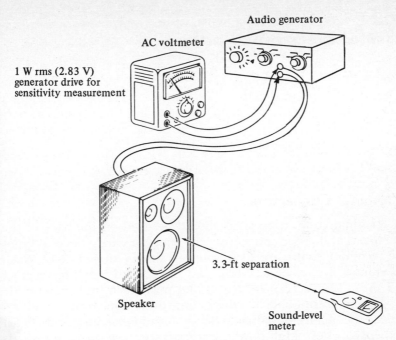

Audio generator

AC voltmeter

1 W rms (2.83 V)
generator drive for
sensitivity measurement

3.3-ft separation

Speaker

Sound-level
meter

Fig. 2-14   Arrangement of equipment for measuring speaker sensitivity.

Driver dB-sensitivity ratings can be used to compare the sound loudness produced by two drivers when using equal power. When the sensitivity of one driver is 3 dB more than the other driver, one driver's sound will seem as though twice as much power is being used. For example, a driver with 93-dB sensitivity will sound noticeably louder than a driver with 90-dB sensitivity.

Midrange and tweeter sensitivity will generally run high (about 94 dB or more) because drivers are very efficient at these frequencies. The sensitivity of the midrange and tweeter drivers should be close (within 3 dB, if possible) to the sensitivity of the woofer. However, if you use a low-sensitivity woofer and a high-sensitivity midrange, you can adjust the loudness of the drivers by using an L-pad with the midrange driver.

2.2
Useful Electronic Parts

Terminal connectors, wire, solder, crossovers, and L-pads are useful in speaker building. The terminals, wire, and solder connect the drivers to the amplifier. Crossovers separate the music signal into separate frequency ranges for the drivers in two- and three-way systems. L-pads provide adjustable loudness control of midrange or tweeter drivers.

Terminal Connectors

A terminal connection strip should be used on the back of the speaker cabinet for connecting the speaker wires. Several types of terminal strips are available, as shown in Fig. 2-15. Push terminals are usually color-coded in red and black for correct wiring and are easy to use. Some push terminals have a recessed mounting block which improves appearance and reduces the chance of damage. Screw terminal strips are the least expensive. Very high power systems often use screw terminals for good contact of the speaker wires.

Phono terminals and plugs are not recommended for speaker connections. If, by mistake, you should connect a speaker wire with a phono plug into an amplifier input jack, serious damage could result to the amplifier.

Wire

Using the right speaker wire will help reduce power loss and provide good electronic damping to the speaker. Wire conductor size is specified with a number such as 14, 16, or 18, which relates to its diameter. As the number becomes smaller, the wire becomes larger and can, therefore, carry more electrical power. When the speaker wire is large (No. 16, for example), more of the amplifier power reaches the speakers. For example: if 40 ft of No. 22 speaker wire is used for an 8-ohm speaker,

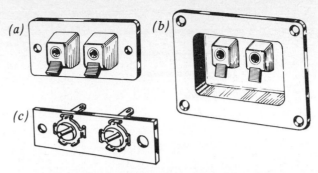

Fig. 2-15 Three common types of terminal strips:
(a) push terminals, flush; (b) push terminals, recessed;
(c) screw terminals, flush.

only about 43 W of a 50-W amplifier will reach the speaker. If larger No. 16 wire was used for this same purpose, about 48 W of the 50-W amplifier could reach the speaker. As you can see, larger size wire reduces power loss.

Larger speaker wire also improves driver damping. The amplifier acts as an electronic "brake" on the driver cone to damp (stop) its motion after the signal changes or stops. When the wire is large and short, the amplifier can more efficiently damp the cone movement. Without this damping, the bass sound may sound mushy or muddy.

For proper operation of your drivers, select your speaker wire size from the chart in Fig. 2-16. Regular No. 16 or 18 lamp wire can be used for speaker wire. It has good insulation, is flexible, inexpensive, and can be supplied by most hardware stores. A clear vinyl plastic-coated wire is also sold by some hardware and electronic suppliers. This wire makes excellent speaker wire if it is No. 18 or larger. Some discount stores also sell a small (No. 22) vinyl-coated wire they call speaker wire, but do *not* use this small wire. Any wire less than No. 18 may noticeably reduce the performance of your speakers.

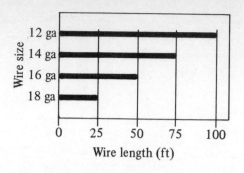

(a) 4-ohm speaker

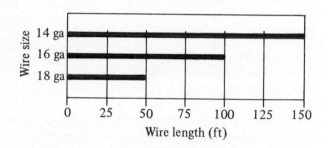

(b) 8-ohm speaker

Fig. 2-16 Charts for selecting the correct wire size in relation to its length between amplifier and speaker.

Solder

Always use *rosin*-core solder for soldering electrical connections inside the speaker. The solder should be $1/16$ in or smaller in diameter and about a 60/40 (tin/lead) type. Each speaker requires just a few inches of solder so only a small roll is needed.

◉ **A WORD OF CAUTION:** *Never* use acid-core solder for electrical work. Both acid-core and rosin-core solder look alike. However, when used, the acid-core solder will quickly corrode electrical wires causing serious damage.

Crossovers

Two typical crossovers are shown in Fig. 2-17. There are three items to consider when selecting your crossover: power rating, crossover frequencies, and crossover slopes.

Power Rating. The power rating of a crossover must be equal to or greater than the power of the amplifier used with the speaker. Crossovers which are too small waste amplifier power. A few of the better crossovers have *circuit breakers* as shown in Fig. 2-18 which protect the drivers when the amplifier power

Fig. 2-17 Two common crossover units.

Fig. 2-18 A three-way crossover
with circuit breaker protection for
the speaker.

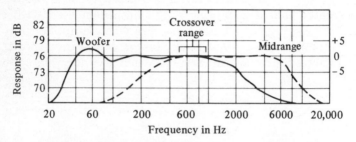

Fig. 2-19 Crossover can occur anywhere within the
frequency range where both drivers are operating at
about equal loudness.

exceeds the crossover rating. These circuit breakers are useful
for those who use high amplifier power and wish to prevent
driver burnout.

Crossover Frequencies. The best crossover frequencies depend on the size and performance of your drivers. Figure 2-19
shows an example of how the frequency responses of two drivers overlap. A crossover frequency can be selected *anywhere*
within a range where both drivers are operating with about

equal output. If the manufacturer suggests a crossover frequency for a driver, try to find a crossover circuit which is close to that frequency. If your drivers have no recommended crossover frequencies, use the following guide to select the crossover:

Two-Way Systems

Woofer Diameter	Suggested Crossover Frequency
8 in	2500 Hz
10 or 12 in	1600 Hz

Three-Way Systems

Woofer Diameter	Suggested Crossover Frequency
8 in	1000/5000 Hz
10 or 12 in	700/4500 Hz
15 in	600/4500 Hz

Of course, you may not find a crossover with the exact frequencies suggested, but anywhere close to these frequencies should produce good crossover performance.

Crossover Slopes.   The slope refers to the ability of the crossover to reduce the signal to the drivers beyond their operating range. The slope (sometimes called *"attenuation"*) is measured by the amount of signal drop in dB per octave.

An *octave* is the range of frequencies equal to one-half or twice some reference (usually the crossover frequency). For example, if the crossover frequency is 800 Hz, then one octave lower would be 400 Hz, and one octave higher would be 1600 Hz, as shown in Fig. 2-20. Crossover slopes of 6 dB and 12 dB are the most common. Figure 2-21 compares a 6-dB and a 12-dB crossover slope.

The 12-dB-per-octave crossovers are suggested for speaker systems. They reduce the woofer power more quickly beyond their range, and, therefore, reduce the chance of a strong low-frequency signal getting into the midrange driver causing it to

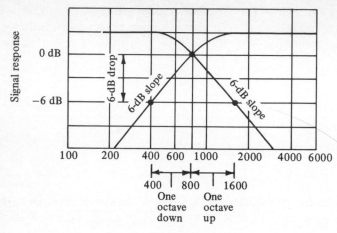

Fig. 2-20 An example of a performance graph of a 6-dB crossover showing the 6-dB slope (drop) per octave.

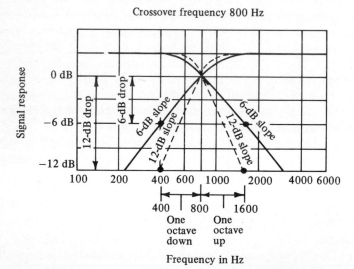

Fig. 2-21 A comparison between 6-dB and 12-dB per octave crossover slopes. Notice how the 12-dB slope reduces the signal faster beyond the crossover point.

Fig. 2-22 An L-pad control
for adjusting driver loudness.

burn out. The 12-dB-per-octave crossover may be slightly higher-priced, but it will provide better protection for your midrange and tweeter drivers.

L-Pads

Midrange and tweeter drivers are usually more efficient than woofers and sound louder in a speaker system. You can reduce treble in a speaker with your amplifier tone control. However, with L-pads, you can adjust and balance the sound of the midrange and tweeter drivers to match the listening room acoustics and your personal listening taste.

L-pads, as shown in Fig. 2-22, are inexpensive and easy to install. However, be sure to select L-pads which have power ratings at least equal to the drivers being controlled.

2.3
Selecting the Cabinet Wood

Speaker cabinets not only affect sound performance but also the appearance of your stereo system and listening area. The cabinet actually becomes a piece of furniture in your room. Selecting good building material is the first step in making your cabinet strong and attractive.

The wood materials for speaker cabinet building are also used in home construction and can be found in most local lumber yards. Many lumber suppliers will offer helpful advice and assistance in selecting quality materials if you briefly explain your project to them in a friendly attitude. Look for quality and do not accept material that has scratches which cannot be sanded out, serious chips, cracks, or warps. Remember, your project will never be any better than the materials you use.

Plywood

Hardwood veneer plywood is one of the best materials for cabinet construction. Birch, oak, and walnut are the most common hardwood veneers used on the surface of the plywood. This type of plywood is strong, flat, and very attractive when finished. There is also a hardwood veneer particle board which looks similar to plywood on the surface, as shown in Fig. 2-23. However, plywood is slightly better because it is stronger and will hold nails or screws better.

Full-size sheets are 48 in by 96 in in size. You should obtain the ¾ in thickness. You may want to plan other projects or share the plywood with a friend if you need only part of a full sheet. Watch for an attractive grain pattern when selecting plywood. Be careful when you transport and cut the plywood so it does not become scratched or damaged.

A softer fir plywood is also available at about half the price.

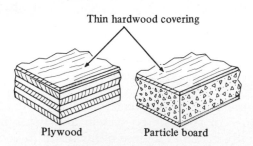

Thin hardwood covering

Plywood   Particle board

Fig. 2-23 Examples of hardwood plywood and hardwood veneer.

This lower grade of softer plywood, however, will sometimes have open (void) areas in the plys. The open areas will not hold nails or screws which may cause construction problems.

Particle Board

One of the big advantages of *particle board* is that it is inexpensive; it may cost only one-fourth as much as hardwood plywood. Also, it is dense with no cracks, grain, or open areas. Since there is no grain pattern, the parts can be laid out in any direction.

To save money, particle board is often used for the grille frame, back, bottom, and driver mounting board. In fact, some builders use particle board for the complete cabinet. The appearance of a complete particle board cabinet can be improved by covering it with hardwood veneer, vinyl cloth, contact paper, wraparound grille cloth, plastic laminates, or paint.

Two grades of particle board are produced. Most lumber suppliers stock the standard-density grade which is called "particle-board underlayment." It is often used by home builders as a top layer floor material. The high-density grade is slightly stronger and designed for cabinet work. When the high-density particle board is not available, most speaker builders use the standard-density particle board with very good results. The standard size of a full particle board sheet is 48 in by 96 in (4 ft by 8 ft). The most common thicknesses are ⅜ in, ½ in, ⅝ in, and ¾ in. You should use the ¾ in thickness for most cabinet parts.

Boards

Boards are used to make battens to hold the screws and nails for the inside joints. Pine boards ¾ in thick are suggested since they are inexpensive, easy to cut, and resist splitting when driving nails or screws. Most lumber yards have a good supply of pine with several widths available such as 3½ in, 5½ in, 7½ in, 9½ in, and 11½ in. The length can be bought in multiples of 2 ft such as 4, 6, or 8 ft. Boards also come in grades such as:

No. 1 and Select	Very clear boards with no knots or defects
No. 2	Some small knots which are tight
No. 3	Many small knots or a few large knots which are tight
No. 4	Many knots with some loose and open knots or cracks and defects

Since No. 1 is the most expensive, No. 2 pine can be used for the battens with good results. However, do not use No. 3 or No. 4 because the defects and knots may cause construction problems. Pine boards can also be used as a speaker cabinet. The knotty-pine look is attractive and enjoyed by many.

Most lumber suppliers also have a small selection of hardwood boards such as oak, birch, mahogany, or walnut. These hardwoods make excellent sides and tops for the smaller speaker cabinets. Boards do not work as well for larger cabinets because of the edge gluing necessary to produce a panel as wide as the cabinet.

◈ **A WORD OF CAUTION:** Make sure that all of your boards are very dry. If you notice any pitch from the boards, do *not* use them. Moisture in boards will cause them to shrink as they dry which may create defects in your cabinet. If possible, use *only* boards which have been *kiln dried*.

2.4
Other Building Items

The smaller building items can be found at local hardware stores and lumber yards, or you may have many of them in your own home or shop.

Small Hardware

The small hardware fasteners such as screws, nails, and staples are an important part of speaker building. Fasteners of the correct style and size will produce a strong speaker cabinet.

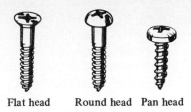

Flat head   Round head   Pan head

Fig. 2-24   Three common types of wood screws which have Phillips slotted heads.

Wood Screws.   Flat head wood screws, as shown in Fig. 2-24, are used for fastening the driver mounting board to the cabinet. Flat head or round head wood screws are used to fasten the L-pads, terminal strip, drivers, and crossover. Some builders use pan head (sheet metal) screws in place of wood screws which work equally as well. If the screw heads will be seen from the front, you may want to paint the heads black before installing. Screws with Phillips-style heads are slightly better than regular heads because the screwdriver will not slip off as easily, but regular slotted heads are okay. Check your speaker material list for exact sizes. If you are designing your own cabinet, here are some suggested sizes:

Driver mounting board	1¾ in No. 8 flat head
Tweeter and midrange driver	¾ in No. 6 round head
Terminal strip	½ in No. 4 round head
Crossover	½ in No. 6 round head
Woofer driver	¾ in No. 8 round head or pan head

Washers.   Small washers are used between the crossover and mounting board at each mounting screw location. The small washers should be rubber to resist vibration and prevent electrical shorts on the under side of the crossover. Most hardware stores have small rubber washers in several sizes, or the rubber washers used in water faucets can be used.

Machine Screws. Round head machine screws can be used to mount the larger woofers. Machine screws with a washer and nut provide a secure mounting for the heavy woofer. Suggested size when using a ¾-in-thick mounting board is 10 × 24 by 1¼ in. Nuts of the same size and small washers are also needed.

Nails. *Finishing nails* are used for most speaker construction. Nails are measured in sizes called *"penny"* which relates to their length as shown by Fig. 2-25. Here are some suggested sizes when building cabinets from ¾-in material:

⅜-in-thick front edge trim	2-penny (1 in) These small nails are often called brads.
⅝-in-thick front edge trim	3-penny (1¼ in)
Battens	3-penny (1¼ in) Common nails or sheetrock nails are suggested.
Back	4-penny (1½ in)
Sides	6-penny (2 in)

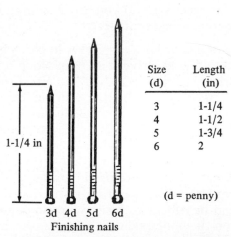

Size (d)	Length (in)
3	1-1/4
4	1-1/2
5	1-3/4
6	2

(d = penny)

1-1/4 in

3d 4d 5d 6d
Finishing nails

Fig. 2-25 Finishing nails for building speaker cabinets.

Staples.   Staples are used to fasten glass fiber and grille cloth. For strength, use the heavier builder's staples which are driven with a staple gun as shown in Fig. 2-26, and not the light office type. A length of $^5/_{16}$ in is suggested. If you do not have staples, small tacks such as carpet tacks or thumb tacks can be used, but they are not as easy to install.

Construction Supplies

The items needed to complete construction will vary slightly depending on the speaker design. The items described in this section are commonly used in building most speakers.

Glue.   A good-quality wood glue is important for strong joints and construction. The yellow carpenter's wood glue shown in Fig. 2-27 is best for cabinet construction. It can be cleaned from your hands and tools with water before it sets, and it is about twice as strong as the white vinyl glue. Powdered wood glues are strong, but must be mixed with water and must be used within about 20 minutes to prevent the glue from hardening in the mixing container.

Fig. 2-26   A heavy-duty staple gun.

Fig. 2-27   Carpenter's yellow wood glue for cabinet construction. (*Borden, Inc.*)

Caulking Compound.   Caulking compound seals the cabinet to prevent air leaks which reduce performance. A good-quality latex caulking compound is suggested since it spreads easily and can be cleaned off hands or tools with water. A caulking gun will be needed for applying caulking compound.

Damping Material.   Glass fiber is suggested to damp the inside of the speaker cabinet. Electronic supply stores often sell what they call *"acoustic fiberglass"* which is 1 in thick. This glass fiber is packaged in a small, convenient size as shown in Fig. 2-28. To save a little money, you can buy your glass fiber from a lumber supplier. They may have a broken package of home insulation, as shown in Fig. 2-29, and will sell you one or two sections (called "batts") for a discount price. A full package of glass fiber would be enough for a dozen or more speakers, so you may not want that much. Home glass-fiber insulation is usually 3½ in or 6 in thick. However, the fiberglass can be easily pulled apart to a thickness of 1 in to 2 in for your speakers. Also, it can be easily cut to size with a scissors.

◆ **A WORD OF CAUTION:**   Glass-fiber material is actually composed of small sharp fibers of glass and it can be irritating to skin, eyes, and throat. To prevent irritation, wear gloves, goggles, and a dust mask when cutting and handling glass-fiber material.

If you are allergic to glass fibers, try using the thick, 1-in polyester or cotton batting designed for making bed quilts. Many fabric stores and home merchandise catalogs have this material. It will be slightly more expensive than glass fiber, but the sound performance will be about equal and it will not irritate your skin. Other materials such as foam insulation for home construction or polyurethane foam for upholstery cushions will not damp the sound enough and are not suggested.

Grille Cloth.   The grille cloth must be attractive, but it must also be an open weave to let the high-frequency sound through. Special grille cloth is sold at some electronic stores, but you

Fig. 2-28 Small packages of glass fiber available from electronic supply stores. (*Radio Shack Division, Tandy Corp.*)

Fig. 2-29 Home insulation glass-fiber material which can also be used for speaker building. (*Owens-Corning Fiberglass Corp.*)

may be able to find similar and less expensive cloth at local fabric stores. Look for a cloth which has a loose thread weave. There should be enough small openings in the weave so you can see objects in the room when you hold a single layer of cloth close to your face. Do not use the very thin sheers, however, because they will allow the drivers to show through.

Cloth with large lines in its pattern is sometimes difficult to install while keeping all lines straight. Cloth without a definite pattern is the easiest to install. Select a color which adds to the appearance of your cabinet wood. Beige, dark brown, or black are often used for speaker grille cloth.

A special sculptured foam grille in black or brown color, as shown in Fig. 2-30, is also sold in some electronic stores. A foam grille is attractive and easy to cut and install. No wooden grille frame is needed when using a foam grille. It can be cut with a scissors or sharp utility knife.

Hook-and-Loop Material.   The grille frame can be held to the mounting board by the use of *hook-and-loop material* (Velcro). Only small pieces are needed in each corner. You can buy hook-and-loop material at some electronic supply stores and at most fabric stores. Black-colored material is suggested as it will be less noticeable on the driver mounting board. The small pieces of hook-and-loop material sometimes have an adhesive back-

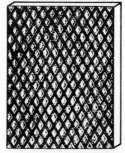

Fig. 2-30   Sculptured foam for the speaker grille.

ing, or they can be cemented in place with epoxy glue. Five-minute epoxy is suggested for faster setting time.

Wood Filler.   Many types of wood filler are available to fill nail holes and other small open areas in the wood. Most fillers are a soft paste which is applied, allowed to dry, and sanded smooth. Read the label and notice if the filler can be stained to match the cabinet wood.

Another type of wood filler is a small putty stick. Putty sticks, as shown in Fig. 2-31, are easy to use *after* the wood has been stained and *one* coat of clear finish has been applied. The stick is rubbed into the area to be filled, and the second coat of clear finish is then applied to the speaker. Take along a sample piece of stained wood when selecting the putty stick color so you will have a good color match.

Sandpaper.   *Aluminum oxide sandpaper* is suggested because it wears longer. Use a grit of about 100 for rough sanding and 150 or 220 grit for finishing sanding of surfaces. A grit of 220 can also be used to lightly sand the first coat of clear finish for

Fig. 2-31   Putty sticks which are used to fill nail holes and wood cracks.

a smoother final appearance. You will need about one sheet of 100 grit, one sheet of 150 grit, and one sheet of 220 grit for each speaker.

◈ **A WORD OF CAUTION:** Do *not* use steel wool for any speaker cabinet work. Steel wool fibers can be left in or around the cabinet. Later, the steel fibers can be pulled into the magnet area of the drivers. When the fibers get near the voice coil and magnet, they may cause serious noise distortion. A driver with this problem *cannot* be repaired. Many builders have learned this important lesson after damaging their woofer driver. Once again, do *not* use steel wool!

Weather Stripping.   *Weather stripping* is a soft foam rubber strip used to provide a removable seal between the cabinet and driver mounting board. Look for a thin strip of ⅛ or ³/₁₆ in thickness and ⅜ to ½ in width. Use the self-adhesive type which is often supplied in rolls as shown in Fig. 2-32.

Fig. 2-32   Weather stripping which is used to seal driver mounting board.

Finishing Materials

Speaker finish does not usually affect the sound. However, a speaker which has a professional-looking cabinet *seems* to work better and is, therefore, more enjoyable. The materials used to finish a cabinet depend upon the appearance desired.

Contact Paper.   Low-cost speakers can be covered with an adhesive contact paper. Most hardware stores and discount stores sell contact paper in 18-in widths and you can buy any length. Many decorative and wood grain patterns are available. It is easy to use, inexpensive, and looks good.

Oil Stain.   Oil stain is the most beautiful and professional wood finish for hardwood cabinets. It brings out the natural grain appearance of the wood which many people enjoy. Oil stain is easy to apply and can be obtained in many colors. The type of wood you are using may slightly affect the final color of the stain. When buying oil stain, take a scrap of cabinet wood with you. Have the salesperson try a few drops of your selected stain on the wood to check its exact color. Oil stain covers a large wood area so you will only need a small can.

A "gel" stain is sold by some stores which is similar in thickness to sour cream. It is easy to apply because it will not drip and also has the advantage of not spilling if the can is tipped. The deep penetrating oil stains (Mini-wax and Watco for examples) produce a slightly more even-colored surface which is less likely to show scratches because of its deep penetration.

Tack Cloth.   After sanding, staining, or varnishing, a dust film is often left on the speaker cabinet. A special tack cloth, as shown in Fig. 2-33, should be used to wipe the cabinet surfaces and remove the dust. Any dust on the surface will cause the final finish coat to be rough. The tack cloth is slightly sticky and picks up dirt and dust from the cabinet surface. A clean surface is very important to a smooth final finish.

Fig. 2-33 A tack cloth for removing dust from cabinet surface before applying finish.

Clear Finish.   A clear coat of finish will help protect the cabinet surface from moisture and dirt as well as make the cabinet easier to clean. Several types of clear finish are available such as wood oils, polyurethane, Deft, varnish, and others.

Wood oils produce a dull, but rich, appearance. They are handrubbed onto the wood surface with a small cloth. Several coats are necessary for protection of the wood.

Of all the clear finishes, polyurethane is one of the most popular because of its hard surface and easy application. Quick-drying finishes such as Deft and One-Hour dry quickly so dust will have less chance to settle on the wet finish. Most clear finishes can be used to cover oil-stained wood, but always check the directions on the can or ask the supplier for advice. Experiment on a small sample of scrap wood if you are not sure.

Many finishes are described as being either "satin" or "glossy" which relates to their appearance. The satin finishes have less shine, and thus are not as likely to show small scratches. A satin finish is often used on high-quality furniture. Glossy finishes have a "wet," shiny appearance which some people prefer.

Paint. The main items to be painted are the grille frame, screw heads, and, sometimes, the driver mounting board. The paint should be flat black to match the color of the driver cones. Using a spray can is the easiest and quickest painting method. One can should be enough for many speaker grilles and all the screw heads. Latex paint is also easy to use and your brush (or hands) can be cleaned with soap and water. Oil or enamel paint will produce a very durable finish, but both require special paint cleaning solvents to clean the brush.

Only the cloth side of the grille frame has to be painted. One coat will cover well enough to hide the light-colored wood frame under the grille cloth. The driver mounting board can also be painted black unless it has a hardwood finish. The black appearance will give the speaker a finished look when the grille is removed.

2.5
Useful Tools

All of the tools used for speaker building are common woodworking tools as shown in Fig. 2-34. The following tools are suggested:

Work Table
> (or two saw horses and plywood or boards to make at least a 2- by 3-ft work surface)

Tape Measure
> (retractable steel tape measure or folding ruler)

Carpenter's Square
> (or metal straight edge at least 12 in long)

Fig. 2-34 The common tools used for building speakers.

Compass

(about 6-in size or larger)

Utility Knife

(or sharp pocket knife)

Wood Chisel

(blade width of ½ or ¾ in)

Wood Rasp

(half-round medium tooth)

Plane

(smoothing or jack plane)

Wood Clamps

(two clamps about 6-in or larger size)

Claw Hammer

(13-oz size is suggested)

Nail Set

(point diameter of $^1/_{16}$ in)

Circular Power Saw

(use a fine-tooth plywood cutting blade)

Sabre Saw

(blade should have about 10 teeth per inch)

Vibrating Power Sander

(straight line preferable or orbital type)

Electrical Hand Drill

(¼- or ⅜-in size)

Drill Bits

(assortment of twist bits from $^1/_{16}$- to ¼-in diameter, ⅜-in spade or twist bit, countersink or multibore bit)

Caulking Gun

(regular size)

Sanding Block

(or wood scrap about ¾ in by 3 in by 4 in)

Paint Brush

(good quality tapered tip about 1½ or 2 in width, poly-foam brushes can also be used)

Scissors

(about 5-in blades)

Staple Gun

(which uses $^5/_{16}$-in staples)

Soldering Iron

(about 30-W soldering iron or 125-W soldering gun)

Screwdrivers

(regular ¼-in blade and/or Phillips No. 2 point, depending on which screws you choose)

Pliers

(long-nose pliers with wire cutter, side-cutting pliers and slip-joint pliers may also be useful)

Work Gloves

(cotton type for handling glass fiber, and rubber or plastic gloves for applying wood stain)

Goggles

(or safety glasses)

Breathing Mask

(inexpensive dust mask)

These tools and items, when properly used, will produce a good-quality cabinet. If you are using a tool for the first time, practice with it on a scrap piece of wood to get the feel of how it works before using it on your speaker. If large power tools are available, the radial arm saw, table saw, and jointer can make the cutting easier and slightly straighter; but they are not required.

Remember, every tool must be kept clean; and cutting tools must be very sharp for best performance, easier use, and safety.

2.6
Speaker Project Plans

Using a set of project plans can save you time, reduce wasted materials, and provide you with many helpful building ideas to make your project better. Plans for five different speakers are shown in this section. They vary in size, power, cost, and performance. A brief description of each speaker is given and followed by a list of materials, construction suggestions, and drawings.

After selecting a speaker plan, you may want to change or adjust some of the sizes or construction methods to suit your tools, skills, and materials. For example, if your board sizes are not quite right for the plan, or you cut a board too small, you can make slight changes in cabinet size. Try to keep the internal volume of the cabinet close to the suggested size. Usually, small changes of less than 10 percent will not seriously affect the sound. Notice in the speaker plans that many of the cutout sizes for the drivers are not shown because different models of drivers are often slightly different in size. You should check each driver size before marking and cutting driver holes.

Speaker Project: Mini-5

This small speaker, as shown in Fig. 2-35, is attractive, easy to build, and produces good sound at low cost. Its simple design and compact size require only a few inexpensive building materials and just one driver.

Typical Speaker Performance: (depending on driver)

Sound loudness:	Moderate (up to 96 dB)
Room size:	50 to 100 ft²
Power rating:	5 to 20 W rms
Frequency response:	110 to 14,000 Hz

Fig. 2-35   The Mini-5 bookshelf speaker.

Material List for Each Speaker:

½-in Particle board (or plywood or boards)
- 2 Sides   5⅞ in × 11⅞ in
- 1 Back   9 in × 11⅞ in
- 1 Driver mounting board   7¹⁵/₁₆ in × 10¹³/₁₆ in
- 1 Top   8 in × 5⅞ in
- 1 Bottom   8 in × 5⅞ in
- 1 Grille frame   7⅞ in × 10¾ in

¾-in Pine board
- 2 Side battens   ¾ in × 10⅞ in
- 2 Top and bottom battens   ¾ in × 6½ in

Hardware
- 14 1-in nails (for battens)
- 32 1¼-in (3-penny) finishing nails (for sides and back)
- 6 1¼-in No. 8 flat head wood screws (for driver mounting board)
- 4 ½-in No. 8 round head wood screws (for driver)
- 40 ⁵/₁₆-in staples (for insulation and grille cloth)

Miscellaneous
- Wood glue (for all wood joints)
- Latex caulking compound (to seal wood joints)
- Glass-fiber insulation, 2 ft², 1 to 2 in thick (for damping material)
- Sandpaper, one sheet 100 grit
- Contact paper, 18 in × 42 in (optional cover for particle board cabinet)
- Wood finishing materials (optional, used only if the hardwood cabinet is built)
  - Wood filler for cracks and nail holes
  - Wood stain
  - Tack cloth
  - Clear wood finish
  - Sandpaper: one sheet 150 grit, one sheet 220 grit
- Flat black paint (for grille frame)
- Grille cloth, 10 in × 13 in
- Masking tape, 1 in wide (for grille frame)

Adhesive foam weather stripping, about ¼ in × ⅜ in × 3 ft (to seal cabinet front)

Hook-and-loop (Velcro) material, ¾ in × 2 in (to hold grille frame)

Five-minute epoxy cement (to fasten hook-and-loop material)

Electronic parts
    1 5-in or other small full-range driver
    1 Terminal connection strip (with mounting screws)
16 in No. 18 lamp wire (for connecting drivers)
6 in Rosin-core solder

Construction Suggestions.   The cabinet parts and grille frame can be cut from one piece of ½-in-thick particle board or plywood 12 in by 48 in. You may find scraps of boards in your shop or near housing projects which are large enough to use for the parts of this cabinet. Even if you use new wood, the material cost will be low. The layout of the particle board pieces is shown in Fig. 2-36. Notice that the two sides are alike and the top and bottom are alike.

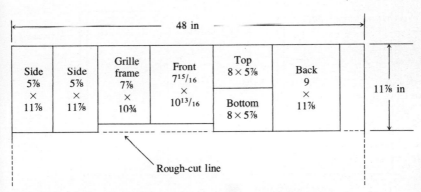

When laying out cutting lines, allow ⅛ in extra at each line where cut will be made for width of saw blade.

Material = ½ in particle board or other wood material.

Fig. 2-36 Parts layout for the Mini-5.

The Mini-5 uses simple construction, as shown in Fig. 2-37. All the joints are butt joints for easy cutting. Battens are used only for the front mounting board. Glue and nail the back directly onto the back side. Since the wood is only ½ in thick, be careful to make sure the nails are driven in straight. After the cabinet is assembled, it can be painted, varnished, or covered with cloth or contact paper. A full-range 5-in driver works best

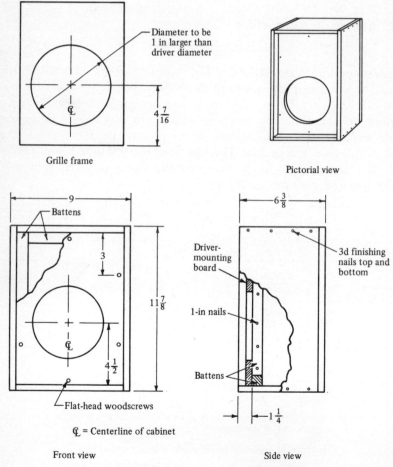

Fig. 2-37   Construction details for the Mini-5.

for this small speaker, but other sizes of small drivers will also produce enjoyable sound. Some builders use automotive stereo speaker drivers, which are about 5 in by 7 in, with good results.

Speaker Project: Compact-8

This 8-in, two-way speaker as shown in Fig. 2-38 is a popular project with many builders. The two drivers provide good frequency response, and its compact size allows it to be used on bookshelves, cupboards, and end tables.

Typical Speaker Performance: (depending on drivers)

Sound loudness:	Strong (up to 105 dB)
Room size:	80 to 190 ft^2
Power rating:	10 to 35 W rms
Frequency response:	80 to 15,000 Hz

Fig. 2-38   The Compact-8 speaker.

Material List for Each Speaker:

¾-in Plywood
- 2 Sides   7⅞ in × 19⅜ in
- 1 Back   10½ in × 18¾ in
- 1 Driver mounting board $10^7/_{16}$ in × $17^{15}/_{16}$ in
- 1 Top   7⅞ in × 12 in
- 1 Bottom   7⅛ in × 10½ in

½-in Particle board
- 1 Grille frame   10⅜ in × 17⅞ in

¾-in Pine board
- 4 Side battens   1 in × 18 in
- 3 Top and bottom battens   1 in × 9 in

¾-in Hardwood board (front edge trim)
- 2 Side edge strips   ½ in × 19½ in
- 2 Top and bottom edge strips   ½ in × 12 in

Hardware
- 16 1-in finishing nails (for front edge trim)
- 30 1¼-in nails (for battens)
- 12 6-penny finishing nails (for sides)
- 18 1¾-in No. 8 (or No. 10) flat head wood screws (for driver mounting board)
- 50 ⁵/₁₆-in staples (for insulation and grille cloth)
- 4 ½-in No. 6 round head wood screws (for mounting cross-over)
- 8 ¾-in No. 8 round head wood screws (for woofer)
- 4 ¾-in No. 6 round head wood screws (for tweeter)

Miscellaneous
- Wood glue (for all wood joints)
- Latex caulking compound (to seal wood joints)
- Glass-fiber insulation, 4 ft², 1 to 2 in thick (for damping material)
- Sandpaper: one sheet 100 grit, one sheet 150 grit, one sheet 220 grit

Wood filler (for cracks and nail holes)
Wood stain
Tack cloth (to remove sanding dust)
Clear wood finish
Flat black paint (for grille frame)
Grille cloth, 12 in × 20 in
Masking tape, 1 in wide (for grille frame)
Adhesive foam weather stripping, about ¼ in × ⅜ in × 5 ft (to seal cabinet front)
Hook-and-loop (Velcro) material, ¾ in × 4 in (to hold grille frame)
Five-minute epoxy cement (to fasten hook-and-loop material)

Electronic parts

1	8-in woofer driver
1	Tweeter driver
1	Two-way crossover (crossover frequency about 2500 Hz, power rating greater than woofer)
1	Terminal connection strip (with mounting screws)
4 ft	No. 16 or No. 18 lamp wire, or similar wire (for connecting drivers)
1 ft	Rosin-core solder

Construction Suggestions. This speaker used ¾-in-thick wood for strong construction and two drivers for good performance. If you are building two speakers and would like to reduce cost, Fig. 2-39 shows a layout pattern for using plywood and particle board. The grille frame should be cut from ½-in particle board. If you would like to use your speakers without a grille and want an attractive hardwood front as shown in Fig. 2-40, use hardwood plywood for all parts.

Speaker construction is simple, as shown in Fig. 2-41. After cutting boards to size, fasten the top, bottom, and back using rabbet joints on the cabinet top to improve appearance and add strength. Notice the batten location as shown in plans. No batten board is to be used on back-bottom joint since the back

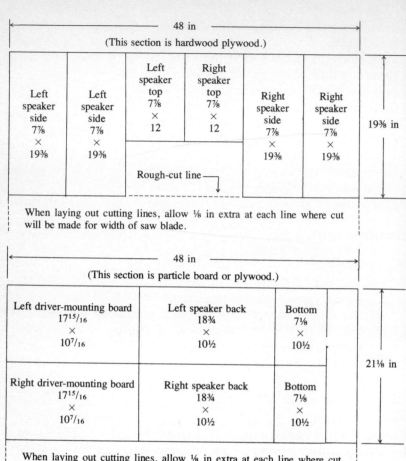

Fig. 2-39 Parts layout for two Compact-8 speakers.

can be fastened directly to the bottom. Be sure to allow time for glue under battens to set before attaching back.

A simple, two-way crossover for the drivers should be used to increase speaker performance. If desired, an L-pad can be installed next to the tweeter on the driver mounting board for control of tweeter loudness.

Fig. 2-40 The Compact-8 with a
hardwood driver mounting board.

Speaker Project: Classic-10

This 10-in, three-way speaker features a full-front grille for
modern classic styling, as shown in Fig. 2-42. Its size is convenient for either bookshelf, table, or floor placement. The full-
front grille is simple in design and easy to build. The driver
mounting board is made from hardwood so the speakers can
be used without grilles if desired. Small size and high performance make this a popular project for many builders.

Typical Speaker Performance: (depending on drivers)

Sound loudness:	Loud (up to 110 dB)
Room size:	110 to 240 ft²
Power rating:	15 to 60 W rms
Frequency response:	60 to 18,000 Hz

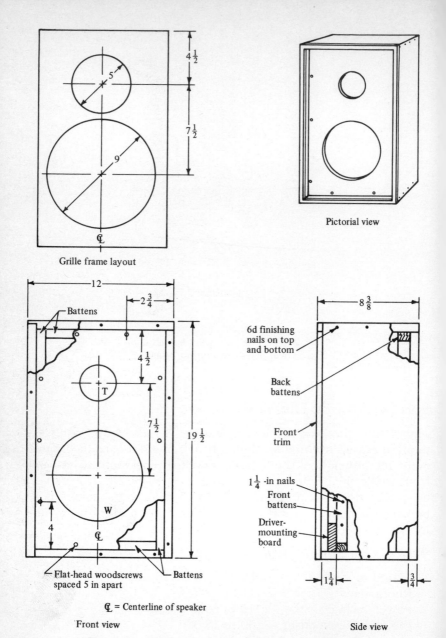

Fig. 2-41 Construction details for the Compact-8.

Fig. 2-42 The Classic-10 speaker.

Material List for Each Speaker:

¾-in Plywood
    2 Sides   10 in × 21⅞ in
    1 Top   10 in × 14½ in
    1 Driver mounting board $12^{15}/_{16}$ in × $20^{7}/_{16}$ in

¾-in Particle board
    1 Back   13 in × 21¼ in
    1 Bottom   9¼ in × 13 in
    1 Grille frame   14½ in × 22 in

¾-in Pine board
    4 Side battens   1 in × $20^{7}/_{16}$ in
    3 Top and bottom battens   1 in × 11½ in

Hardware
    30 1¼-in nails (for battens)
    24 4-penny finishing nails (for back)
    16 6-penny finishing nails (for sides)

10 1¾-in No. 8 flat head wood screws (for driver mounting board)

50 ⁵/₁₆-in staples (for insulation and grille cloth)

12 Speaker driver mounting screws (size and type will depend on the drivers you use)

4 ½-in No. 6 round head wood screws (for mounting crossover)

Miscellaneous

Wood glue (for all wood joints)

Latex caulking compound (to seal wood joints)

Glass-fiber insulation, 7 ft², 1 to 2 in thick (for damping material)

Sandpaper: one sheet 100 grit, one sheet 150 grit, one sheet 220 grit

Wood filler (for cracks and nail holes)

Wood stain

Tack cloth (to remove sanding dust)

Clear wood finish

Flat black paint (for grille frame)

Grille cloth, 18 in × 26 in

Masking tape, 1 in wide (for grille frame)

Adhesive foam weather stripping, about ¼ in × ⅜ in × 6 ft (to seal cabinet front)

Hook-and-loop (Velcro) material, 1 in × 6 in (to hold grille frame)

Five-minute epoxy cement (to fasten hook-and-loop material)

Electronic parts

1 10-in woofer driver

1 Midrange driver

1 Tweeter driver

1 Three-way crossover (crossover frequencies about 700 Hz and 4500 Hz, power rating equal to or greater than woofer)

1 or 2 L-pad controls, if desired (power rating greater than midrange driver)

1 Terminal connection strip (with mounting screws)
10 ft No. 18 lamp wire (for connecting drivers)
18 in Rosin-core solder

Construction Suggestions. The grille frame, back, and bottom are cut from ¾-in particle board as shown in Fig. 2-43. The sides, top, and driver mounting board are laid out and cut from ¾-in hardwood plywood as shown in Fig. 2-44. The driver cutout areas are not marked for exact diameters as they may vary slightly, depending on the driver manufacturer. Always check exact driver diameter before cutting holes.

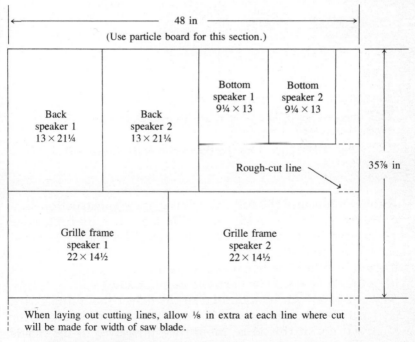

Fig. 2-43 Layout for the particle-board parts, Classic-10.

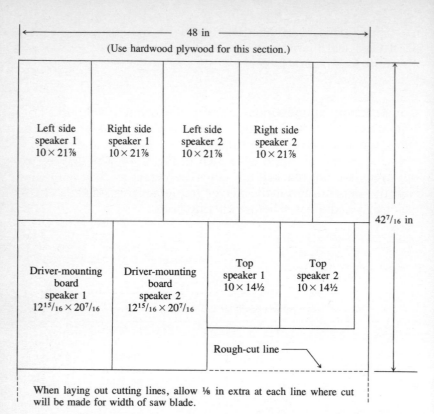

Fig. 2-44 Layout for the hardwood parts, Classic-10.

Rabbet joints and the full-front grille make construction simple, as shown in Fig. 2-45. The grille front has its front edge corners beveled at 45 degrees to add style. This 45-degree bevel also allows the grille cloth to be stretched around the corners without any folded corner seams showing. The bevel can be cut with either a tablesaw or portable circular saw.

The crossover can be mounted to the driver mounting board next to the midrange driver. If you should have a crossover which will not fit this area, mount the crossover to the inside of the cabinet top.

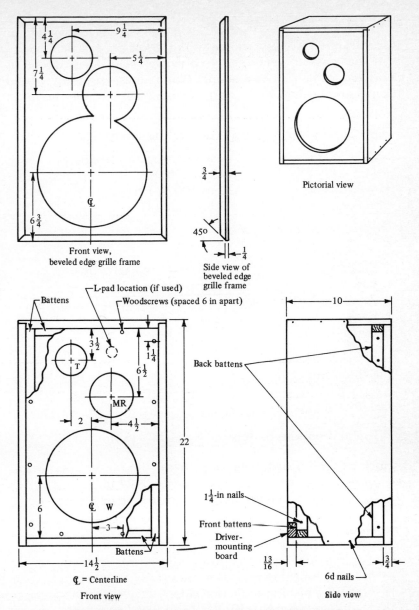

Fig. 2-45 Construction details for the Classic-10.

Speaker Project: Natural-12

This attractive speaker, shown in Fig. 2-46, has excellent sound from low bass to very high frequencies. The 12-in woofer is well-liked for its rich bass sound. Piano notes, especially, sound natural and strong. This is an excellent speaker for the finest music.

Typical Speaker Performance: (depending on drivers)

Sound loudness	Very loud (up to 112 dB)
Room size:	140 to 300 ft²
Power rating:	20 to 100 W rms
Frequency response:	42 to 19,000 Hz

Material List for Each Speaker:

¾-in Plywood

2	Sides	11 in × 23⅞ in
1	Top	11 in × 16 in
1	Driver mounting board	14⁷/₁₆ in × 22⁷/₁₆ in
1	Back	14½ in × 23¼ in
1	Bottom	14½ in × 10¼ in

½-in Particle board

1	Grille frame	14⅜ in × 22³/₈ in

¾-in Pine board

4	Side battens	1 in × 22½ in
3	Top and bottom battens	1 in × 13 in

¾-in Hardwood board (front edge trim)

2	Side edge strips	½ in × 24 in
2	Top and bottom edge strips	½ in × 16 in

Hardware
- 32 1¼-in nails (for battens)
- 14 1-in finishing nails (for front edge trim)
- 24 4-penny finishing nails (for back)
- 16 6-penny finishing nails (for sides)
- 18 1¾-in No. 8 (or No. 10) flat head wood screws (for driver mounting board)

Fig. 2-46
The Natural-12 speaker.

50 $^5/_{16}$-in staples (for insulation and grille cloth)
20 Speaker driver mounting screws (size will depend on the type of drivers you use)
 4 ½-in No. 6 round head wood screws (for mounting cross-over)

Miscellaneous
Wood glue (for all wood joints)
Latex caulking compound (to seal wood joints)
Glass-fiber insulation, 8 ft², 1 to 2 in thick (for damping material)
Sandpaper: one sheet 100 grit, one sheet 150 grit, one sheet 220 grit
Wood filler (for cracks and nail holes)
Wood stain
Tack cloth (to remove sanding dust)
Clear wood finish
Flat black paint (for grille frame)
Grille cloth, 18 in × 26 in
Masking tape, 1 in wide (for grille frame)

Adhesive foam weather stripping, about ¼ in × ⅜ in × 7 ft (to seal cabinet front)

Hook-and-loop (Velcro) material, ¾ in × 4 in (to hold grille frame)

Five-minute epoxy cement (to fasten hook-and-loop material)

Electronic parts

    1 12-in woofer driver

    1 5- or 6-in midrange driver

    1 Tweeter driver

    1 Three-way crossover (crossover frequencies about 700 Hz and 4500 Hz, power rating greater than woofer)

1 or 2 L-pad level controls, if desired (power rating greater than midrange driver)

    1 Terminal connection strip (with mounting screws)

 10 ft No. 18 lamp wire (for connecting drivers)

 18 in Rosin-core solder

Construction Suggestions.   One of the features of this speaker is the hardwood-finished front. This allows you to use the speaker with grille removed as shown in Fig. 2-47. The layout

Fig. 2-47 The Natural-12 speaker with grille removed.

of parts is shown in Fig. 2-48. Particle board is suggested for the bottom and back, or plywood can be used for this also. Notice the suggested rough-cut lines for easier handling.

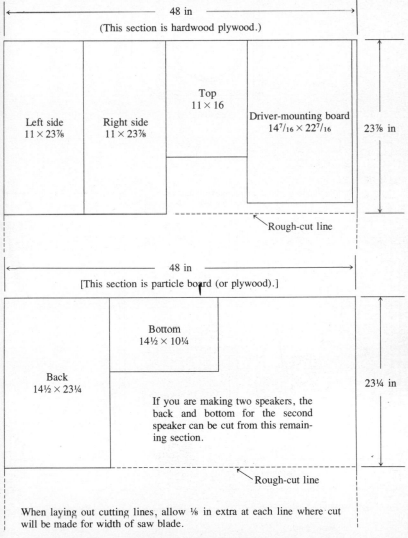

Fig. 2-48   Layout of parts for the Natural-12 speaker.

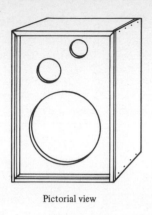

Pictorial view

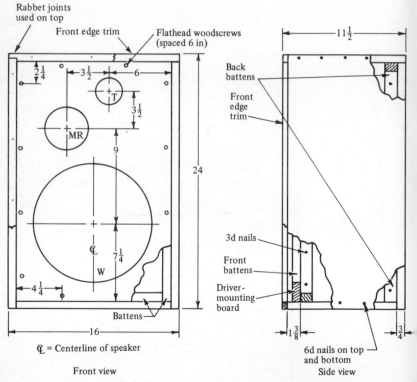

Fig. 2-49 Construction details for the Natural-12.

Speaker construction is based on the plan shown in Fig. 2-49. Rabbet joints are used on the top corners to make construction easy and strong. Note location of batten boards from front and back edges. The front edge trim boards can be made from ¾-in-wide decorative wood trim available from many lumber suppliers. This decorative trim, if used, would replace the ¾-in hardwood edge strips and produce a more custom designed appearance.

Be certain during construction to draw all screws tight so all parts will be secure. The large 12-in woofer produces strong vibrations which may cause "rattle" noises from any loose parts.

Speaker Project: Super-15

If you like strong bass sounds and high-quality performance you will like the Super-15 project, as shown in Fig. 2-50. The large 15-in woofer can handle high power and deliver the deep, low bass sounds. The dual tweeters are an option, but will provide excellent high-frequency coverage.

Fig. 2-50   The Super-15 speaker.

Typical Speaker Performance: (depending on drivers)

Sound loudness:	Super loud (up to 115 dB)
Room size:	180 to 480 ft^2
Power rating:	30 to 150 W rms
Frequency response:	30 to 20,000 Hz

Material List for Each Speaker:

¾-in Plywood
| 2 | Sides | 14½ in × 31⅞ in |
| 1 | Top | 14½ in × 21 in |

¾-in Particle board
1	Back	19½ in × 31¼ in
1	Driver mounting board	30⁷/₁₆ in × 19⁷/₁₆ in
1	Bottom	13¾ in × 19½ in

½-in Particle board
| 1 | Grille frame | 30⅜ in × 19⅜ in |

¾-in Pine board
| 4 | Side battens | 1¼ in × 30½ in |
| 3 | Top and bottom battens | 1¼ in × 18 in |

¾-in Hardwood board (front edge trim)
| 2 | Side edge strips | ½ in × 32 in |
| 2 | Top and bottom edge strips | ½ in × 21 in |

Hardware
- 36 1¼-in nails (for battens)
- 18 1¼-in finishing nails (for front edge trim)
- 50 6-penny finishing nails (for sides and back)
- 50 ⁵/₁₆-in (or ⅜-in) staples (for insulation and grille cloth)
- 16 2-in No. 8 (or No. 10) flat head wood screws (for driver mounting board)
- 20 Speaker driver mounting screws (size will depend on the type of drivers you use)
- 4 ½-in No. 6 (or No. 8) round head wood screws (for mounting crossover)

Miscellaneous
   Wood glue (for all wood joints)
   Latex caulking compound (to seal wood joints)
   Glass-fiber insulation, 12 ft^2, 1 to 2 in thick (for damping material)
   Sandpaper: one sheet 100 grit, one sheet 150 grit, one sheet 220 grit
   Wood filler (for cracks and nail holes)
   Wood stain
   Tack cloth (to remove sanding dust)
   Clear wood finish
   Flat black paint (for grille frame)
   Grille cloth, 24 in × 36 in
   Masking tape, 1 in wide (for grille frame)
   Adhesive foam weather stripping, about ¼ in × ⅜ in × 10 ft (to seal cabinet front)
   Hook-and-loop (Velcro) material, 1 in × 4 in (to hold grille frame)
   Five-minute epoxy cement (to fasten hook-and-loop material)

Electronic parts
        1 15-in woofer driver
        1 Midrange driver
   1 or 2 Tweeter drivers
        1 Three-way crossover (crossover frequencies about 600 Hz and 4500 Hz, power rating equal to or greater than woofer)
        2 L-pad controls (power rating greater than midrange driver)
        1 Terminal connection strip (with mounting screws)
    10 ft No. 16 lamp wire (for connecting drivers)
    18 in Rosin-core solder

Construction Suggestions.   The sides and top can be laid out and cut as shown in Fig. 2-51. The layout for the driver mounting board, bottom, and back is suggested in Fig. 2-52. The grille frame can be cut from a separate piece of ½-in particle board. The location and spacing of the midrange and tweeter drivers

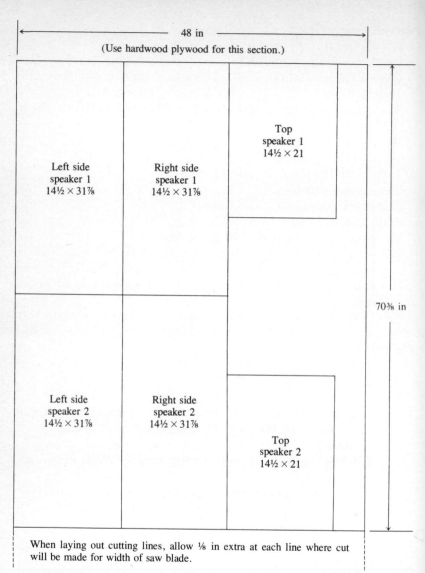

Fig. 2-51 Layout of hardwood parts for two Super-15 speakers.

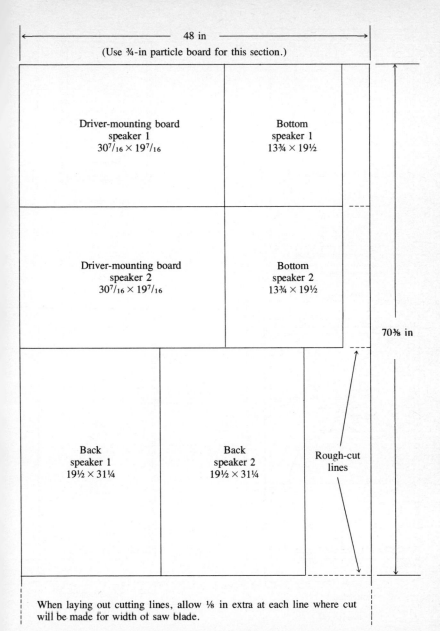

When laying out cutting lines, allow ⅛ in extra at each line where cut will be made for width of saw blade.

Fig. 2-52 Layout of particle-board parts for two Super-15 speakers.

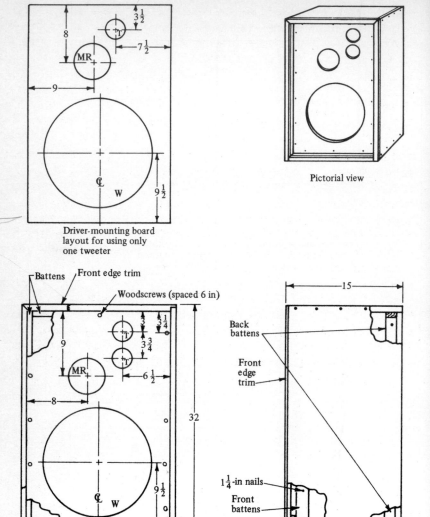

Driver-mounting board
layout for using only
one tweeter

Pictorial view

Fig. 2-53   Construction details for the Super-15.

will depend on the size and number of drivers used. Try to keep the midrange, tweeter, and woofer drivers at least ½ in apart at their mounting flanges. If two or more tweeters are used, they can be as close as $1/16$ in apart but should be positioned one above the other in a vertical arrangement. Try to keep all drivers in a vertical arrangement as much as possible rather than side-by-side. The vertical arrangement allows the sound to spread (disperse) more uniformly across the listening area.

Construction plans are shown in Fig. 2-53. Rabbet joints on the cabinet top make construction simple, yet strong. If you prefer to eliminate the nail holes on the outside of the cabinet, screws and glue blocks can be used to fasten from the inside. When building, be sure to set the battens in the correct distance and allow the glue to dry at least 1 hour before mounting the back. The joints on this large speaker must be glued and fastened very well due to the large vibrations from the woofer which can shake weak joints loose.

When installing the woofer driver, some builders apply a thin bead of clear liquid silicone bathtub sealer under the driver flange. The silicone sealer helps prevent air leaks and serves as an adhesive between the drivers and mounting board. Although this is optional, it will help prevent the woofer from vibrating loose during the extended use of high amplifier power.

CHAPTER THREE

Building Your Speakers

You are now ready to build your speakers. Many suggestions are given in this chapter to make construction easier and better. Begin by selecting quality tools and keep them in good condition. Of course, with any tool, good safety practices must be used to prevent injury.

As you build, be sure to pay attention to all the small details of craftsmanship. Both appearance and sound quality depend on your speaker's construction. Take the time to do each step of construction as well as you can.

Step-by-step instructions and construction methods are given at the end of this chapter. These instructions can be used with any of the suggested speaker plans and will help you do each part in the proper order.

3.1
Safety Suggestions

Building a speaker system is an enjoyable project, but good safety practices are necessary to prevent an accident to you or someone else nearby. It is strongly suggested that you review and use the following safety practices:

1. *Wear Eye Protection.* Use safety glasses or goggles when working with tools and materials. Flying chips can easily get into eyes if no eye protection is used.

2. *Do Not Be Distracted.* Do not talk or watch someone else while you are operating tools. Keep your eyes and mind on the job you are doing. When working with other people, do not allow them to be fooling around near you or your project.

3. *Keep Tools Sharp and Clean.* It may seem strange, but a sharp tool is safer and does better work. Less pressure is needed with sharp tools, and if there is a skin cut, it will heal faster when made with a clean, sharp tool.

4. *Use the Right Tool for the Job.* Be sure to select and use the right size and type of tool for each job. Trying to cut a rabbet joint with a sabre saw, for example, will only cause tool damage, wasted material, and possible injury. If you are not sure which tool to use, ask someone who is more experienced.

5. *Keep Saw Blades at a Safe Height or Depth.* Set the saw blades of circular saws and table saws so they extend only about ⅛ in beyond the wood thickness as shown in Fig. 3-1. Less exposed blades will reduce chances of injury.

Fig. 3-1 For safety, adjust saw blade to extend only about ⅛ in beyond wood surface.

6. *Support the Work Firmly.* Use strong saw horses or a strong table. Injury can result if a section of wood sags and causes a power tool to kick back. Also, a falling cabinet can cause both foot injuries and wood damage.
7. *Do Not Rush.* Plan your project time so you can do each step carefully. Rushing to do a job may cause you to become careless. Remember the old saying, "Haste makes waste."
8. *Use Common Sense.* Think about what you are doing (or going to do). Remember, you are working with expensive materials and power tools, so consider the results of your actions before you do each step or procedure.

3.2
Step-by-Step Building Procedures

The building of your speaker will be much easier if each step of construction is done in the proper order. Step-by-step building procedures and suggestions are given in this chapter and can be used with any speaker plan. If you are building a matched pair of speakers, do the same step on both speakers before going on to the next step.

Lay Out and Cut Parts

The wood parts used in speaker building must be carefully laid out so each piece will fit well during construction. Place your cut lines to take advantage of beautiful wood grain patterns and then doublecheck your measurements. Remember, even the best professional carpenters occasionally make a mistake, so a little extra effort to doublecheck sizes may save time and material.

STEP 1.
Place a Soft Protective Pad on Your Work Table (or Saw Horses).
The wood for your speakers is soft and can be easily scratched. Protect your cabinet wood during cutting and building. Place a folded towel, clean corrugated (brown) cardboard,

a rug, or other similar material on the saw horses or work surface. Do *not* use newspaper. The ink used on newspaper will easily rub off on your boards and leave smudge marks.

STEP 2.
Plan the Layout Arrangement.   Plan the arrangement of each wood part so there will be very little waste of material. Notice how in Fig. 3-2 there are two arrangement examples of the same parts and sizes, with one arrangement requiring a much larger section of wood material and having more waste. If you are using a speaker plan from this book (Chap. 2), an arrangement is suggested in the plans. Be sure to note the wood grain direction as you lay out the sides, top, and front. The finished speaker will look more attractive if the wood grain runs in the longest direction of the speaker sides and top.

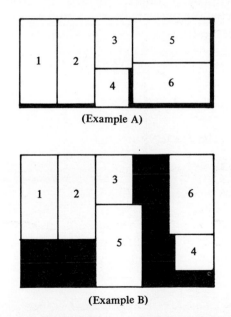

(Example A)

(Example B)

Fig. 3-2 Two arrangements of the same parts to compare material size needed and amount of waste (shown by the black areas).

STEP 3.
Lay Out the Cutting Lines Using the Double-Line Method to Allow for Saw-Cut Thickness. Most saws remove about ⅛ in of wood due to their blade thickness. To cut wood to the correct finished size, lay out each wood piece exactly to its suggested size and allow ⅛ in between pieces. Figure 3-3 shows an example of double-line marking. When cutting, saw between the lines. A small amount of splintering on one surface of the wood normally occurs during sawing. Splintering will not be seen if it is on the side which will be inside the cabinet. Therefore, cuts to be made with a circular power saw or sabre saw should be marked on the *back* side of plywood. Cuts to be made with a crosscut hand saw, table saw, or radial arm saw should be marked on the *front* (best) side of plywood.

STEP 4.
Mark the Rough-Cut Lines. If you are working with full sheets of plywood or particle board, you may want to cut them

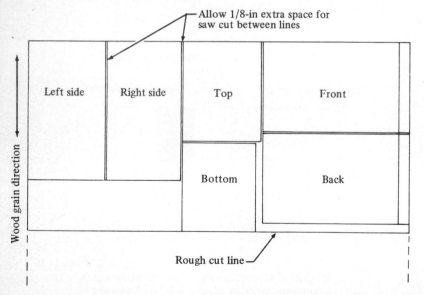

Fig. 3-3   Layout which allows ⅛ in between parts for saw cut.

into smaller pieces for easier handling and cutting. Rough-cut lines are suggested in some speaker plans and can be laid out on the boards as shown in Fig. 3-4. By this method, full sheets can be reduced to two or three smaller pieces with very little wasted material. Be sure to use a very straight board or other straightedge for marking rough-cut and all other lines.

STEP 5.
Knife-Cut the Plywood Before Sawing.
Plywood may splinter as you saw across grain. To reduce splintering, use a utility knife (or sharp pocket knife) and metal straightedge to make a cut about $1/16$ in deep exactly on the line as shown in Fig. 3-5. Knife-cut both lines before sawing between lines.

STEP 6.
Use a Power Saw to Cut Cabinet Sides, Top, Front, Bottom, and Back.
Support the wood securely before sawing to prevent pinching of the blade which causes kick-back. Saw between the cut lines (if you are using the double-line method) or to the outside (waste area) of a single line. If you have used the knife-cut method, any splinters which start should break off at the cut-line for a smooth edge corner as shown in the top ex-

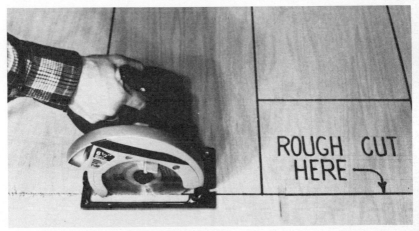

Fig. 3-4 Layout of rough-cut lines for easier saw cutting.

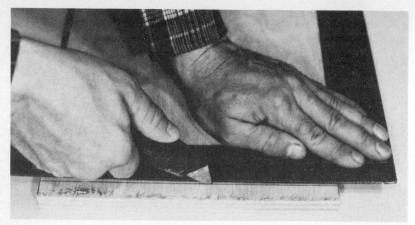

Fig. 3-5 Knife-cutting plywood to reduce splintering.

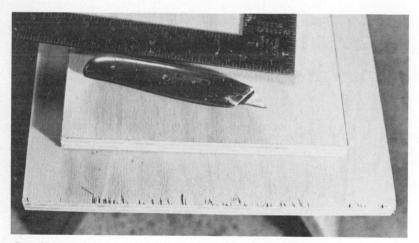

Fig. 3-6 Comparison after sawing of a knife-cut plywood (top) to a plywood with no knife cut.

ample of Fig. 3-6. The bottom example shows the plywood with no knife-cut before sawing and it has, therefore, become badly splintered after sawing. After all pieces have been cut, check each piece for correct size. Make any necessary size corrections.

STEP 7.
Cut Rabbet Joints in the Top Section (If They Are to Be Used on Your Cabinet). Rabbet joints are strong and professional-looking. They are easy to cut with a table saw by making one saw-cut for the depth and one with the board up on edge for the thickness. You can also cut a rabbet joint with a circular saw by marking a line on the back side of the wood which is equal to the wood thickness (usually ¾ in). Set the saw blade for the depth of the rabbet cut (which will leave about ⅛ in of material) as shown in Fig. 3-7. The rabbet cut is now made by sawing several cuts next to each other between the wood edge and ¾-in marked line. Experience has shown that the rabbet joint will fit slightly better if you make the saw-cut nearest the line first; then start from the outer edge and work inward. Smooth the bottom of the cut with a wood chisel or 100 grit sandpaper.

STEP 8.
Mark and Cut the Batten Boards. Check the material list for the number and size needed. Mark the width and length of each batten on the ¾-in-thick No. 2 pine board. Battens may

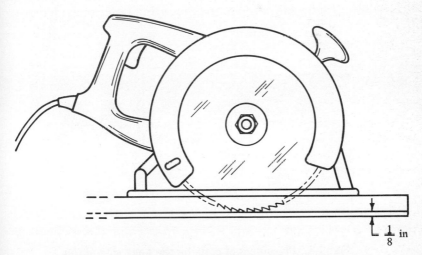

Fig. 3-7 Setting of the saw blade to cut a rabbet joint.

be marked ½ in longer than specified and trimmed to exact necessary size later during assembly. Use the circular power saw (or table saw if available) to cut each batten strip.

STEP 9.
Cut the Front Edge Trim.   The front edge trim should be cut from a piece of hardwood which matches the cabinet plywood sides. Some wood suppliers sell decorative trim which you can also use as edge trim. The trim should be ¾ in wide by about ½ in thick. The length will depend on the type of corner joints used. Cut the trim to a rough length now; then recut to exact length later during installation.

STEP 10.
Design Your Own Driver Arrangement.   To arrange your own driver placement, place the drivers face down on the back side of the driver mounting board. Carefully arrange the drivers so their flanges are about ½ in or more apart and at least 1 in or more from the nearest mounting board edge as shown in Fig. 3-8. Place the midrange driver (if one is used) between the woofer and the tweeter. Arrange the drivers so they will be in (or near) a vertical row after the speaker is completed and standing upright. Mark the screw mounting holes of each driver.

Fig. 3-8 Placement of parts on the back side of the driver mounting board.

To locate the centers of drivers on the mounting board, remove the drivers and draw diagonal lines across the screw mounting holes as shown in Fig. 3-9.

STEP 11.
Lay Out the Driver Mounting Holes. The exact size of a driver mounting hole can be found by measuring the driver mounting flange width on the back side as shown in Fig. 3-10.

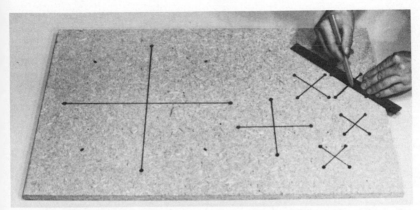

Fig. 3-9 Driver screw locations are marked and crossed to find the center of the driver hole to be cut.

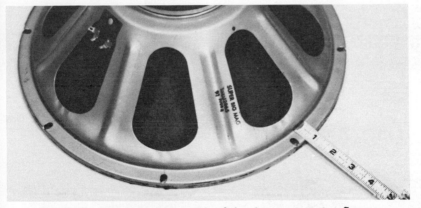

Fig. 3-10 Measuring the width of the driver mounting flange.

Then measure the exact driver diameter on the front side. Double the flange measurement and subtract it from the exact driver diameter. For example, if a woofer has a flange of ⅝ in and measures exactly 12¼ in in diameter, the correct mounting hole size would be 11 in (⅝ × 2 = 1¼ in; then 12¼ − 1¼ = 11-in cutout diameter). Use a pencil (or drafting) compass such as shown in Fig. 3-11 to lay out hole diameter. If a very large driver diameter must be drawn, a large compass can be made from a small stick with two small holes drilled and spaced equal to the radius (one-half the diameter). Place a nail through one hole into the center of the driver mounting hole and use a pencil in the other hole to draw the circle as shown in Fig. 3-12. Some tweeters have small terminals on each side. These tweeters need two extra cutouts to allow room for both terminals as shown in Fig. 3-13.

STEP 12.
Marking the L-Pad Locations. The L-pads are usually installed in a convenient area near the midrange or tweeter drivers on the driver mounting board. If the mounting board area is crowded, the L-pads can be installed on the cabinet back near the terminal connection area. Their exact location on either

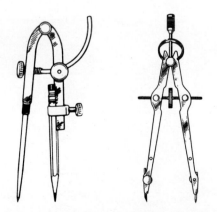

Fig. 3-11 Examples of two types of compasses for laying out driver holes.

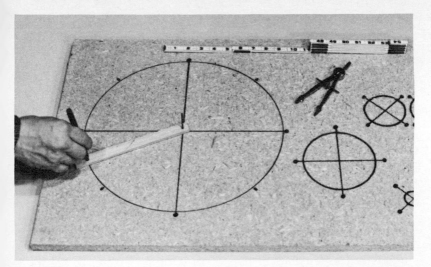

Fig. 3-12   Large driver holes can be laid out with a handmade compass stick.

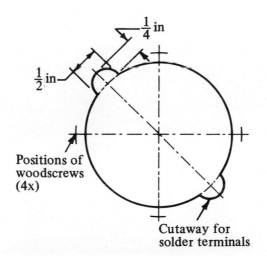

Fig. 3-13   Suggested cutout for tweeter driver to allow for terminals.

of these boards does not affect performance. Some L-pads require only a ⅜-in or ½-in hole, while others require larger cutouts. Locate and mark the holes for each L-pad.

STEP 13.
Lay Out the Grille Frame.   The grille frame has cutout areas for each driver and L-pad. The centers of the cutout areas can be marked by placing the grille frame board *under* the driver mounting board. Align the two boards and hold or clamp them securely to prevent their shifting. Use a small (¹⁄₁₆-in diameter) bit and drill through both pieces of wood at the center of each driver and L-pad location as shown in Fig. 3-14. The grille frame driver holes can now be laid out. Using a compass, mark diameters for the driver and L-pad cutout areas about ½ in larger than the outer diameter of each driver or L-pad. Try to keep the grille frame edges at least 1 in wide for strength. Figure 3-15 shows how the cutout areas of a grille frame often overlap.

STEP 14.
Lay Out the Terminal Connection Opening.   Terminal connections are usually centered on the back board of the speaker

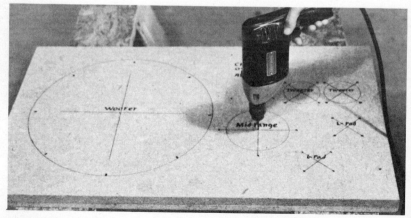

Fig. 3-14   Place the grille frame under driver mounting board and mark center locations of parts by drilling with small drill bit.

and near (about one-fifth of the height) up from the bottom. To lay out the cut lines, measure the terminal connector and determine its mounting hole size. Now find the desired location for the terminal connector on the back board and mark the cutout area. If you are using a flat strip terminal connector, you can recess the strip by using a small piece of scrap wood (about 4 in × 4 in) for a terminal mounting board as shown in Fig. 3-16. Cut or drill out the area on the terminal mounting board where the solder terminals of the terminal strip will be located so the wire connections can be made. Fasten the terminal strip to the small mounting board with screws. Now, find the desired location and lay out a small area about 2 in by 2 in on the cabinet back where the terminals are to be later installed.

STEP 15.
Cut the Mounting Holes.   A sabre saw is used for cutting the mounting holes. Use a blade which has about 10 teeth per inch as shown in Fig. 3-17. To start a cut, a small hole of about ⅜-in diameter should be drilled on the inside of any areas to be cut out as shown in Fig. 3-18. This hole will allow the sabre saw blade to be inserted for beginning the cut. Cut on the inside of the line as shown in Fig. 3-19. After cutting holes, check the sizes by putting your drivers and other parts in the holes.

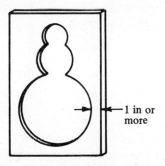

Fig. 3-15 Overlapping driver areas of grille frame.

1 in or more

Fig. 3-16 Using a small board on the inside of the cabinet back for recessing a flat terminal strip.

Fig. 3-17 Sabre saw blade
with about 10 teeth per inch.

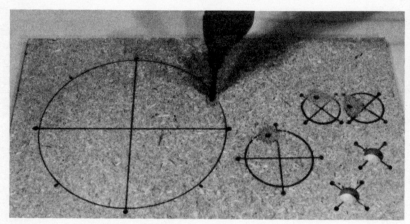

Fig. 3-18 Drill holes to start sabre saw blade.

If the parts will not fit because the holes are slightly small, try enlarging the holes slightly with a wood rasp or the sabre saw.

STEP 16.
Check Your Parts. At this point, all of your speaker parts should be cut. Figure 3-20 shows the parts of a speaker which are cut and ready for assembly.

Fig. 3-19   Insert blade and cut on inside edge of hole lines.

Fig. 3-20   Wood parts which will make a complete speaker cabinet.

Assembly of Parts

Check to make sure each part fits correctly before applying glue. Fasten all wood parts together securely so vibrations from the woofer will not cause cabinet noises. Sealing wood joints with caulking compound prevents noise from air leaks during use.

STEP 17.

Start Finishing Nails.   The sides (or other parts) can often be assembled easier if the finishing nails are started first as shown in Fig. 3-21. Finishing nails hold well and leave only a small hole in the wood surface, but they often crack hardwood boards when driven. To reduce cracking, drill small holes for the nails about the same size as the nail or just slightly smaller. If you do not have a drill bit, a finishing nail with its head removed can be used as a drill bit.

◈ **A WORD OF CAUTION:** Do *not* drill so deep that the drill chuck leaves a mark on the wood surface.

STEP 18.

Apply Wood Glue.   Wood glue is used to give extra strength to the cabinet joints. Apply just a small bead (about ⅛ in wide) of glue to the joint before installing fasteners as shown in Fig. 3-22. If too much glue is used, it will squeeze out and leave a mess on the wood. Wipe off any extra glue with a damp rag

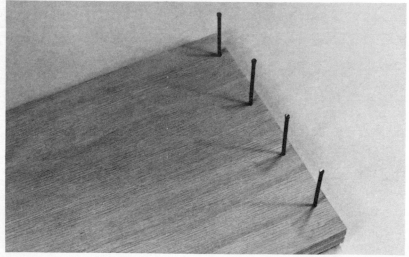

Fig. 3-21   Start finishing nails.

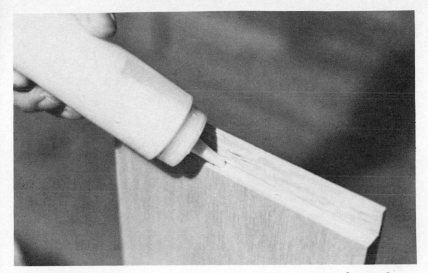

Fig. 3-22   Apply glue to cabinet joints which are being fastened.

and later sand the remaining glue off after it has dried. Spilled glue will not take a stain and will leave light-colored marks on the finished wood unless it is removed by sanding. Wet glue can be cleaned from hands or tools with warm water and a paper towel or rag.

STEP 19.
Assembly of Sides, Top, and Bottom.   Fastening the wood pieces will be easier if you have someone hold the parts while you drive the nails or install glue blocks. (If you are using glue blocks, follow Steps 20 and 28.) To install nails, place the cabinet top board vertically on a table as shown in Fig. 3-23. Apply glue and place the cabinet side in correct position. Drive the two outer edge nails in first so the heads are only out of the wood about $^1/_{16}$ in. Check the boards for correct inside corner squareness by using a small square as shown in Fig. 3-24. Drive the remaining finishing nails. Now, use a nail set as shown in Fig. 3-25 and drive (set) each nail head about $^1/_{16}$ in below the surface. Install the bottom section in a similar manner. When

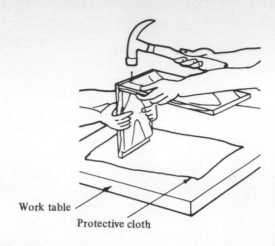

Work table

Protective cloth

Fig. 3-23 Method of holding parts to begin assembly.

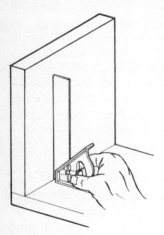

Fig. 3-24 Check corner squareness during assembly.

Fig. 3-25 Drive finishing nails 1/16 in below wood surface with a nail set.

all nails are driven and set on the first side, turn the cabinet over and fasten the other side in place with glue and nails. Be sure to keep padding under the cabinet to protect the wood surfaces.

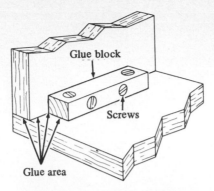

Fig. 3-26 Glue blocks can be used to improve the strength of corner joints.

STEP 20.
Install Glue Blocks (Optional).   Glue blocks and screws can be used in place of nails for inside corner joints where the sides, top, and bottom cabinet parts meet. These blocks take more time to install, but they are strong and give a professional appearance. The blocks are about ¾ in by ¾ in in size. The length of the glue blocks should be cut to fit between the front and back batten boards. Wood screws are fastened into both panels of wood as shown in Fig. 3-26. The screws should be spaced about 3 in apart on each side of the block. A screw size of 1¼-in No. 8 will work well for ¾-in-thick wood parts. If you use larger glue blocks, adjust the screw length accordingly. See Step 28 for suggestions on installing wood screws.

STEP 21.
Install the Batten Boards.   Check the speaker plan to determine batten board location. Mark the required locations on the inside of the sides, top, and bottom as shown in Fig. 3-27a. Remember, some of the plans do not use a batten on the back-bottom joint. Hold the battens in place and check for correct length. Apply a small bead of glue to each batten and fasten in place with 1¼-in nails (for ¾-in plywood cabinets). Space the

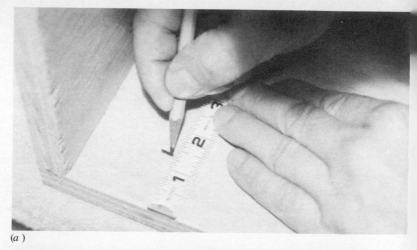

(a)

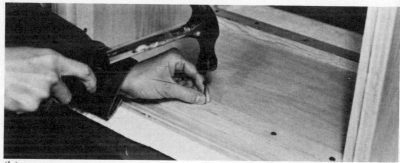

(b)

Fig. 3-27 (a) Mark the location of batten boards. (b) Installing batten boards.

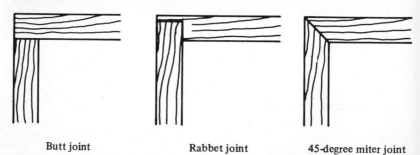

Butt joint   Rabbet joint   45-degree miter joint

Fig. 3-28   Three common types of wood joints.

nails about 4 in apart as shown in Fig. 3-27b. Install the side battens first, then the top and bottom battens. Allow at least 1 hour for the glue to dry before installing the back panel.

STEP 22.
Install the Front Edge Trim.
The corners of the front edge trim can be either 45-degree miter joints or butt joints as shown in Fig. 3-28. The miter joints look more professional than the butt joints if they are cut accurately. The butt joints are easier to make and are often used by beginners.

After deciding which corner joints to use, place edge trim boards on cabinet front; then mark and cut the exact length needed. Install the front edge trim boards on cabinet using a very small bead of glue and small finishing nails (brads) spaced about 6 in apart. Any glue which squeezes out may leave glue stains, so only a small amount of glue should be used. Use a nail set to set the finishing nail heads below the surface.

STEP 23.
Caulk the Battens.
Apply caulking compound to the *inside* seams of the speaker batten boards and other *inside* joints as shown in Fig. 3-29. Do *not* apply caulking to outside batten seams.

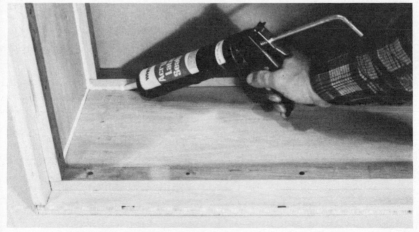

Fig. 3-29   Caulking inside batten and cabinet joints.

STEP 24.
Install the Back Panel.   Place the cabinet with its front edge trim down on a cloth or cardboard. Check the size of the back panel by placing it into its mounting area. Make any size adjustments to the back with a wood rasp, saw, plane, or sandpaper. Now install the back to the cabinet by applying glue to the battens and fastening the back with finishing nails spaced about 4 in apart. Set the nail heads below surface.

STEP 25.
Caulk the Back Panel.   Apply caulking compound to the inside cabinet seams where the battens meet the back.

STEP 26.
Fill the Nail Holes and Cracks.   If a paste wood filler is to be used, it should be applied to nail holes and cracks at this time and allowed to dry.

STEP 27.
Sand the Cabinet Surfaces and Edges.   After construction, the corners and edges should be sanded with a medium 100 grit sandpaper. You can make a sanding block from a scrap of wood. Place the sanding block inside a piece of sandpaper and sand in the direction of the wood grain as shown in Fig. 3-30. Do *not* sand across the grain, or the sandpaper will leave scratches on the wood surface. An electric oscillating sander can also be used as shown in Fig. 3-31. Be careful when sanding sharp corners. If you apply too much pressure, the cabinet corner will tear the sandpaper. When all of the visible scratches, saw marks, and defects have been removed, switch to a 150 or 220 grit sandpaper and sand all outer cabinet edges and surfaces again until they are very smooth. Wipe or brush the dust off and use a bright light to check for glue spots, scratches, or other defects. Repair any defects in the cabinet surfaces if possible.

◗ **A WORD OF CAUTION:**   Do *not* sand the plywood surface too much in one spot or you might sand right through the thin veneer outer layer.

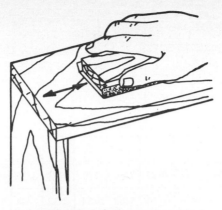

Fig. 3-30   Use of the sanding block.

Fig. 3-31   A vibrating power sander and touchup hand sanding block.

STEP 28.
Suggestions for Using Wood Screws.   Wood screws hold very well in wood. They are used with glue blocks, drivers, electronic parts, and for fastening the driver mounting board to the cabinet. Wood screws must be installed correctly to prevent wood cracking, damaged heads, or stripped threads. To install screws, a pilot hole and a shank hole must be drilled. Figure 3-32 shows an example of a wood screw and the proper pilot and shank hole sizes. Drill a shallow shank hole first; then drill a

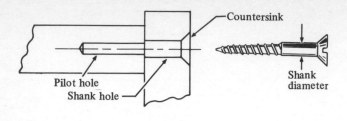

Countersink

Shank
diameter

Pilot hole

Shank hole

No. of screw	1	2	3	4	5	6	7	8	9	10
Shank	5/64	3/32	3/32	7/64	1/8	9/64	5/32	11/64	11/64	3/16
Pilot	–	1/16	1/16	5/64	5/64	3/32	7/64	7/64	1/8	1/8

Fig. 3-32 Chart showing suggested drill bits for wood screw pilot and shank holes.

pilot hole as deep as the screw is long. If the screw is flat-headed, a countersink hole must also be drilled on the top edge to fit the screw head. Use a countersink bit as shown in Fig. 3-33. A special drill bit for screws called a multibore bit can be used to drill the shank, pilot, and countersink holes all at one time as shown in Fig. 3-34. To drive screws, place a small amount of wax or bar soap on the threads for lubrication and use a proper size screwdriver. The screwdriver blade should have sharp edges on the tip and should fit the screw slot as shown in Fig. 3-35. Many builders prefer Phillips head screws since the screwdriver will not slip off the head as easy. Be sure to draw all screws equally as tight for even pressure.

STEP 29.
Drill the Driver Mounting Board Screw Holes. Place the cabinet on the work table with its front side up. Set the driver mounting board into its front mounting area of the cabinet. Make any necessary adjustments to its size so the fit is close, but not tight around the edges. Place the drivers and other parts into their mounting holes. Using a pencil, mark the screw locations of each part. Also mark the screw locations which hold

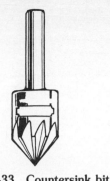

Fig. 3-33   Countersink bit.

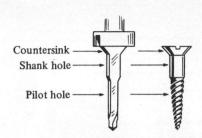

Countersink
Shank hole
Pilot hole

Fig. 3-34   Multibore bit.

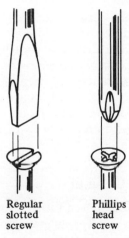

Regular
slotted
screw

Phillips
head
screw

Fig. 3-35   Proper fit
of a screwdriver.

the mounting board to the cabinet as shown in Fig. 3-36. Note
the suggested screw spacings in the speaker plans. A 6-in spacing is average on many speakers. Remove the drivers and use
the correct size shank, pilot, and countersink drill bits or multibore bit to drill each of the screw holes.

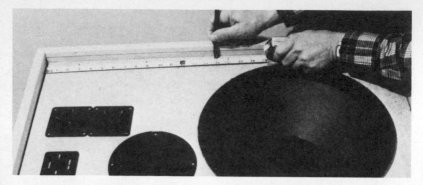

Fig. 3-36   Marking of the driver mounting board screw location.

STEP 30.
Check the Grille Frame Size.   The last woodworking step in building the cabinet is to check the grille frame. Place the grille frame on top of the driver mounting board as shown in Fig. 3-37. Make any necessary size corrections so the grille frame has about $1/16$-in clearance between each of its edges and the cabinet walls. Also check size and location of cutout areas for drivers and other parts. Mark the front of the grille frame so you can later identify and paint the front side black.

Apply Finish to the Cabinet

After constructing the cabinet, a finish should be applied to the outer surfaces to improve appearance and protect the wood. Inexpensive finishes such as paint, contact paper, or vinyl cloth can be used on a particle-board cabinet. If you have a hard-wood cabinet surface, you can apply an attractive finish by using oil stain and a clear finish. Each type of finish has certain advantages. When selecting the finish, consider the ease of use, protection, cost, and most important, the appearance.

STEP 31.
Paint the Grille Frame and Driver Mounting Board.   The grille frame should be painted flat black on the front side so it

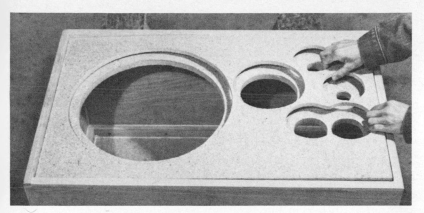

Fig. 3-37   Checking the grille frame size.

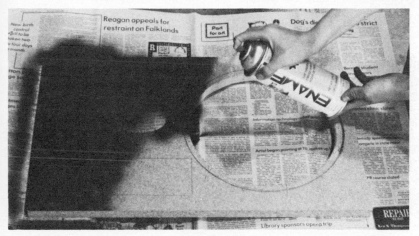

Fig. 3-38   Spray painting the front of a driver mounting board.

cannot be seen through the grille cloth. Place newspaper or scrap boards under the parts to be painted to protect the work area and surfaces. Use a spray paint, as shown in Fig. 3-38, or an enamel or latex paint. Paint the front surface and the edges inside the cutout areas. One coat will usually be enough. If the driver mounting board is particle board, its front surface should also be painted flat black for a more professional look.

STEP 32.
Paint Screw Heads.   The screws used for mounting the drivers, L-pads, and driver mounting board should have their heads painted flat black to match the color of the drivers. To paint screw heads, make a holding board from a scrap of wood or cardboard. Drill the necessary number of holes close together using a bit which is slightly larger than the screw threads. Place the screws in the holes and spray the heads as shown in Fig. 3-39.

STEP 33.
Apply Contact Paper (Optional).   A small particle-board cabinet as shown in Fig. 3-40 can be easily and cheaply covered with contact paper. However, the cabinet should first be given one coat of clear varnish so the contact paper will stick better. Mark the paper so it will extend up the side, across the top, and back down the other side. Allow 2 in extra to hold onto the bottom. Also allow 3 in extra in width to fold onto the back and around the front edge. Cut the paper with a scissors. When installing contact paper keep it tight to prevent wrinkles as shown in Fig. 3-41. Remove only enough backing to do one cab-

Fig. 3-39   Spray painting screw heads black.

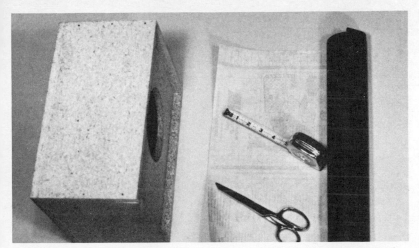

Fig. 3-40 A small particle-board speaker which will be covered with contact paper.

Fig. 3-41 Applying contact paper to the speaker.

STEP-BY-STEP BUILDING PROCEDURES **135**

inet side at a time. Work out any air bubbles by rubbing toward the edge of the cabinet. Use a scissors or a straightedge and sharp knife as shown in Fig. 3-42 to trim contact paper.

STEP 34.
Apply Oil Stain to the Cabinet Wood.   The most attractive finish is an oil stain applied to a hardwood surface. The natural beauty of the wood will make your speaker equal to other fine quality furniture. The following suggestions should give you excellent results.

- Before applying stain, place the cabinet on cardboard or old cloth so that any spilled stain will not damage the work surface.
- To prevent stains on clothing, wear a shop apron or other work clothes. Use rubber or plastic gloves on your hands to prevent stains.
- The stain should be stirred or shaken well before using (except gel stain). Use a small cloth or paint brush (about 1½ to 2 in wide).
- If you have never used oil stain before, practice applying it on some scraps of wood.
- Wipe stain onto the wood as shown in Fig. 3-43. Work the stain into all corners of the front cabinet area.

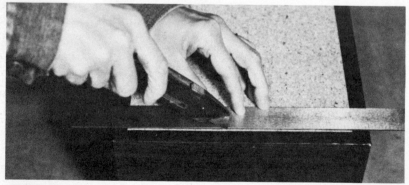

Fig. 3-42 Trimming contact paper with a sharp utility knife and metal straightedge.

Fig. 3-43 Applying wood stain to the cabinet.

- After applying stain to one speaker, use a cotton cloth to wipe all stained surfaces and remove excess stain before applying stain to second speaker.
- Always wipe in the direction of the wood grain. Turn the wiping cloth often for better use. Use a screwdriver to work the wiping cloth into the inside corners of the cabinet front as shown in Fig. 3-44.
- After wiping the stain off, check the stained surface for defects.
- If the stain appears too dark, uneven in color, or if some areas need more sanding, the stain should be removed immediately with a cotton cloth soaked in turpentine. This will lighten the stain color, make it more even in color, and make

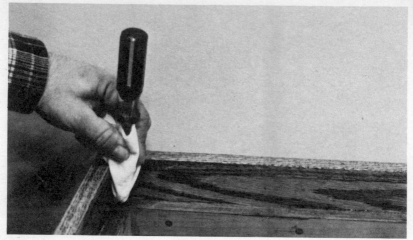

Fig. 3-44   Use a screwdriver and rag to remove extra stain from corners.

it possible to sand without plugging the sandpaper so quickly. After removing the stain by wiping with turpentine, repair any defects, and allow the cabinet to dry for 24 hours. Then apply another coat of stain (only if you have removed the first coat) and wipe dry as before. If just part of a board is darker, it can sometimes be lightened by wiping in the grain direction with a cotton cloth which is only damp with turpentine.

- After applying stain, clean your brush by dipping it in turpentine or paint thinner and squeezing out the remaining stain, as shown in Fig. 3-45. Repeat cleaning procedure until brush is clean.

- Allow at least 24 hours (48 hours are suggested) for stain to dry (at room temperature) before applying clear finish. The stain may look dull after drying, but the clear finish will bring back the rich look of the wood grain.

STEP 35.
Apply the First Coat of Clear Finish.   A clear finish will help bring out the real beauty of the wood grain, as well as provide a protective layer to prevent smudges and dirt stains.

Fig. 3-45 Cleaning your brush.

A warm area (about 70°F) which has clean air is needed for applying wood finish. Use a good-quality clear finish from a new or clean can. If the can has been used before and has a dry skin over the liquid or appears to be lumpy or dirty, do *not* use it. Dirt or lumps in a clear finish will leave a rough surface on your project. After opening the can, use a small paper cup or the bottom half of a regular paper cup as a dipper. Remove enough finish to do just one speaker, as shown in Fig. 3-46. Place the finish in a clean small can and save the dipper as you may need more finish later to complete both speakers.

Dust may have settled on the cabinet surfaces while the stain was drying. Remove dust by wiping all finished surfaces with a tack cloth just before applying the clear finish. Use a good-quality brush which has a tapered tip as shown in Fig. 3-47 for applying finish. Do not use a cheap brush because it may shed loose hairs, leaving them in your finish. The new polyfoam brushes work well and will give a smooth finish. Always brush in the direction of the wood grain, as shown in Fig. 3-48, using smooth, long strokes. After brushing a surface, check the edges around the surface for any run-over finish which can be smoothed out with the brush. Apply a coat of finish to the front surface of the front batten boards which will later hold the weather stripping.

Fig. 3-46 Use a small cup to dip varnish from the can.

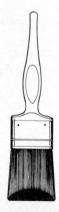

Fig. 3-47 A high-quality brush with a tapered tip.

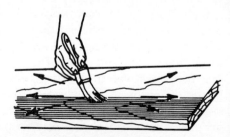

Fig. 3-48 A method of brushing to prevent brush marks.

When both speakers have been finished, do *not* pour remaining finish back into the new can. This remaining finish will have small pieces of dust in it which would contaminate the new finishing material. The remaining finish should be either covered with a plastic wrap (Saran wrap, for example) and saved for another project or discarded. The brush can be cleaned in paint thinner or lacquer thinner, depending on which type of finish you use. Check the directions on the can for the best cleaner. The polyfoam brushes are usually discarded.

STEP 36.
Apply the Second Coat of Clear Finish.　After the first coat of finish has dried 24 hours or more at room temperature (70°F), the cabinet is ready for the second coat. However, if you are using putty stick nail hole filler, it should be used before the second coat of finish is applied. Rub the putty stick material into each nail hole and crack until it is filled, as shown in Fig. 3-49. Rub any extra putty off the wood by using a clean cotton cloth.

Before applying the second coat of finish, sand the dried first coat lightly with a sanding pad of extra fine (220 grit) sand-

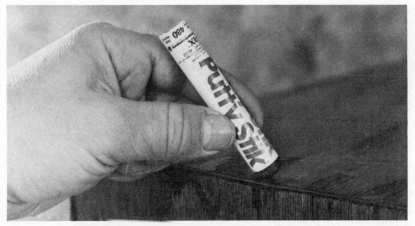
Fig. 3-49　Filling nail holes with a putty stick.

paper. The sanding pad can be made by folding the sandpaper in half twice as shown in Fig. 3-50. Do *not* use steel wool as it may later cause damage to the drivers. Use the sanding pad to *lightly* sand all large surfaces removing any roughness in the finish. Sand only enough to make the surface smooth. Be careful not to sand the edges or corners too much or you will sand right through the first coat and into the raw wood. Stop sanding as soon as all the surfaces feel smooth. After sanding, wipe all surfaces with a tack cloth to remove dust. Apply the second coat of finish in the same manner as the first coat.

Final Assembly

The cabinet is now ready to be completed by mounting and wiring electronic parts, installing insulation, and attaching the grille cloth.

STEP 37.
Install the Drivers. The drivers are usually mounted from the front side of the mounting board, as shown in Fig. 3-51, to give a slight increase in cabinet volume and for better high-frequency performance. Figure 3-52 shows how the dispersion (spreading of sound) becomes wider when the driver is mounted on the front. The woofer requires large wood screws or machine screws for a secure mounting. Figure 3-53 shows how a

Fold sandpaper as shown to make a finished sanding pad.

Fig. 3-50   A folded sanding pad for lightly sanding the first varnish coat.

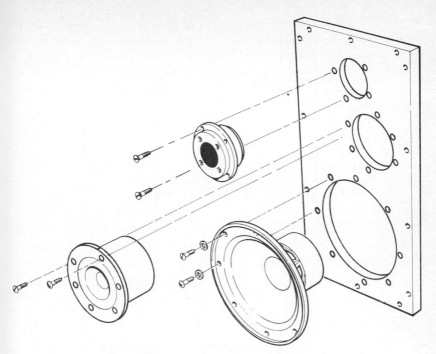

Fig. 3-51 Front mounting of the drivers.

machine screw, washer, and nut should be installed if that combination is used.

To install drivers, use the screws which were painted black earlier. A very small bead of caulking compound or silicone can be used under the woofer flange to help seal the system if desired. Draw all screws equally tight for even pressure. When the driver is mounted from the front as suggested, the paper gasket serves no useful purpose. The gasket is used in some designs where the drivers are mounted from the back side.

◆ **A WORD OF CAUTION:** Be careful so the tools do not slip and damage the cones as shown in Fig. 3-54. When installing drivers, the powerful magnets sometimes pull the tools and cause a tool to slip off the nut or screw.

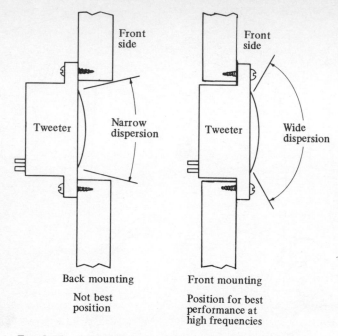

Fig. 3-52 A comparison of dispersion angles when tweeter drivers are mounted in either the back or the front of the driver mounting board. For high frequencies, front mounting is best.

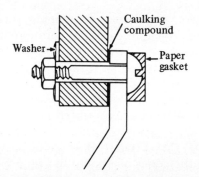

Fig. 3-53 A machine screw and nut for driver mounting.

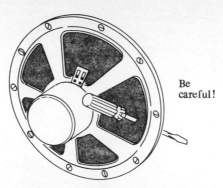

Be careful!

Fig. 3-54 Use caution when tightening screws on the driver so the screwdriver will not slip and damage the cone.

STEP 38.
Mount the Crossover.   The crossover should be mounted to the back side of the driver mounting board if space is available, as shown in Fig. 3-55. If there is not enough room, the crossover can be mounted on the inside of the cabinet top. This top area is preferred over other cabinet surfaces because it will have *no* glass fiber covering later. Do *not* mount the crossover to center area of the back panel as this area often vibrates during loud music and the vibrations may shake the crossover loose. When you mount the crossover, place a small washer (plastic or rubber is suggested) between the crossover and the speaker cabinet at each mounting screw as shown in Fig. 3-55. This washer will provide a small space for the wires under the crossover and prevent bending or cracking of the crossover board.

STEP 39.
Install Damping Material (Glass-Fiber Insulation or Polyester Batting).   Glass-fiber insulation consists of many small, sharp fibers. To prevent skin or body irritation, you should wear gloves, goggles, and a dust mask when cutting or handling it. The damping material will only be installed on the sides, back,

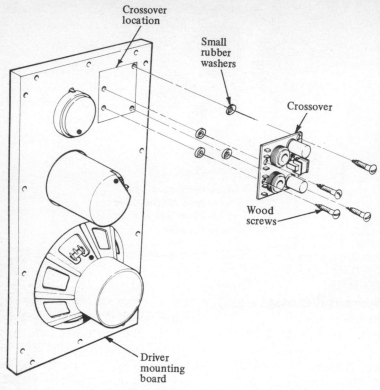

Crossover
location

Small
rubber
washers

Crossover

Wood
screws

Driver
mounting
board

Fig. 3-55   Mounting of the crossover.

and bottom of the cabinet. There is *no* damping material on
the top since it may shake loose from there and fall onto the
woofer cone causing distortion or damage. Separate the insulation into layers about 1 to 2 in thick. Use a scissors, as shown
in Fig. 3-56, to cut the sides, back, and bottom. Use a staple
gun to fasten the insulation inside the cabinet, as shown in Fig.
3-57. Place staples about 6 in apart along the edges and in 6-in
rows across the center area.

STEP 40.
Install the Terminal Connection Strip.   Place the cabinet with
its front side down on a cloth or cardboard to protect the front

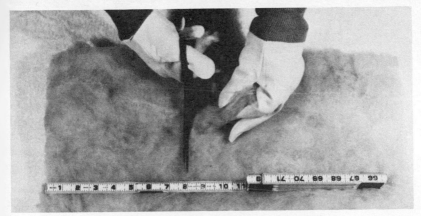

Fig. 3-56 Cutting of glass-fiber insulation.

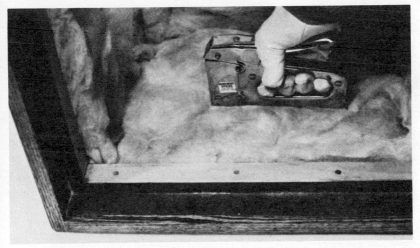

Fig. 3-57 Install the glass-fiber material with a staple gun.

edge trim. Install the terminal connection strip on the back using small wood screws, as shown in Fig. 3-58. Terminal strip connectors which are mounted to a terminal mounting board are installed from the inside of the cabinet. To install these connectors, use four small wood screws (one near each corner) to fasten the mounting board in place.

Fig. 3-58   Installing the terminal connection strip.

STEP 41.

Install the Weather Stripping.   Adhesive foam weather stripping is used to seal the driver mounting board to the cabinet. The adhesive surface will stick better if the batten boards were given one coat of clear finish earlier. To apply the weather stripping, cut it to length with a scissors and press it in place along the outer edge of the batten boards, as shown in Fig. 3-59. The top and bottom pieces should butt up against the side pieces for a good seal. The paper backing can be peeled off after the weather stripping is fastened to the wood.

Electrical Connections

Electrical connection of speaker parts is simple, yet important to performance. Only a few connections are necessary and they are easy to solder.

STEP 42.

Identifying Driver Terminal Polarity.   Driver terminal *polarity* refers to the positive "+" or negative "−" driver terminals which are connected to the voice coil inside. Knowing which terminal is positive and which is negative is necessary when making the wire connections to the crossover (which also has

Fig. 3-59   Apply weather stripping to the front batten boards.

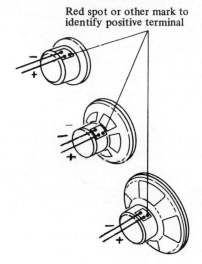

Red spot or other mark to
identify positive terminal

Fig. 3-60   Terminal marking.

positive and negative terminals). The positive terminal is usually labeled with a "+" sign, red color, or a red spot, as shown
in Fig. 3-60. The negative terminal is labeled with a "−" sign
or black color. If there is no marking, you can find the positive
terminal by using a C or D cell battery. Using two wires, con-

nect the battery to the driver terminals for a few seconds and notice if the cone moves in or out. If the cone moves *out*, the terminal which is connected to the positive end (projected end) of the battery is the positive driver terminal. If the cone moves *inward*, the driver terminal which is connected to the negative end (flat end) of the battery will be the positive driver terminal.

STEP 43.
Determine Speaker Impedance. Most amplifiers are designed for speakers which have 4- to 16-ohms impedance with 8 ohms being standard. The impedance of a speaker will be determined by the number of drivers, their impedance, and the way they are connected. If you use only one driver in the woofer, midrange, and tweeter sections, there should be no impedance problems. However, if two tweeter drivers are used in each speaker, the impedance of the tweeter section will not be the standard 8 ohms.

Figure 3-61 shows two examples of driver connections in speakers. The first example shows two 8-ohm drivers connected in series which equals 16-ohms impedance. The second example shows the same two 8-ohm drivers connected in parallel which equals 4-ohms impedance. In a three-way system, using two tweeter drivers, the 4-ohm parallel connection will draw more amplifier power and thus sound louder than the 16-ohm series connection. The parallel connection is recommended for two midrange or tweeter drivers when louder sound is desired from those drivers.

STEP 44.
Correct Soldering Procedures. You are now ready to make the wire connections by soldering. The following suggestions will help you develop good soldering skills:

- Use *only* rosin-core solder which has been designed for electronic work.
- Use a soldering gun or small electric soldering iron with a clean tip.
- If the tip is dirty or corroded, use aluminum oxide sandpaper or an emery cloth to clean the tip surfaces. Then heat the tip and apply fresh solder so the tip surfaces are completely

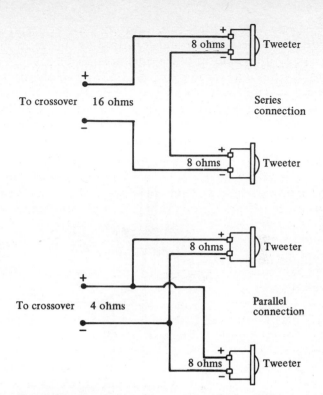

Fig. 3-61 Examples of connections for two tweeter drivers in one speaker.

coated. Excess solder on the hot tip can be removed by wiping the tip on a damp paper towel or sponge. The soldering iron (tip) is now ready for use.

- Do *not* solder over any material (carpet, good clothing, etc.) which may be damaged by a falling drop of hot solder.
- Stranded wire used for speaker work should be *tinned* so it will not fray (develop loose strands). To tin a wire, first re-move wire insulation; then twist the loose strands to form a tight wire end. Heat the wire end with the soldering iron. Hold some solder on the wire until the solder melts and flows in and around the strands; then remove the soldering iron.

- When two or more wires are connected to one terminal, you should wrap the wire around terminal as shown in Fig. 3-62 so wires will be held in place during soldering.
- To solder the wires, refer to Fig. 3-63. Place the flat surface of the soldering iron tip on the connection of the wire and the terminal. Apply rosin-core solder to the terminal and wires until the solder melts and produces a smooth solder flow over the wire-terminal connection. Remove the solder-

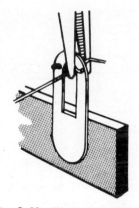

Fig. 3-62 Wrapping of wires on terminal before soldering.

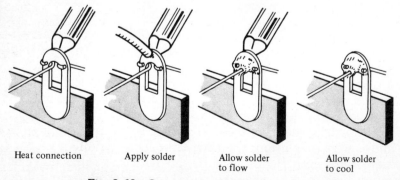

Heat connection   Apply solder   Allow solder to flow   Allow solder to cool

Fig. 3-63 Suggested soldering procedure.

ing iron from the terminal. Do *not* apply solder to the tip of the iron and then spread it over the connection.

- Allow a few seconds for the solder to cool before working with the connection and wires. You may notice the solder change from a shiny to a dull appearance as it cools.

- Carefully inspect all solder connections. If the solder does *not* have a smooth flow appearance, reheat the connection and apply slightly more solder. Do *not* keep your soldering iron on a connection any longer than required to flow the solder onto the terminal and wires. Extra heating time may melt insulation on the wire or cause other damage.

- If you are just learning the soldering skill, take a few minutes and practice soldering with a few scraps of wire. NOTE: In soldering, the important principle to remember is that the connection is supposed to melt the solder. The purpose of the soldering iron is to heat the connection to a temperature hot enough to melt solder.

STEP 45.
Connect the Drivers and Crossover.   Use No. 18 lamp wire (or similar wire) for all connections. If you have just one driver in each speaker, the driver terminals can be directly connected to the terminal strip on the back of the speaker. If you are using a two-way or three-way system, the drivers are connected to the crossover.

A typical three-way crossover is shown in Fig. 3-64. Notice the terminal markings. The terminal marked "COMM" or "−" is to be connected to all of the negative driver terminals (unless you are using series wiring as explained in the previous section on impedance). The terminals marked "W," "MR," and "T" must be connected to the positive terminals of the woofer, midrange, and tweeter drivers as indicated by the letters.

The connections to the crossovers are usually made by soldering directly to the terminals. Quick-disconnect terminals, as shown in Fig. 3-65, are convenient if the wires will be removed at some future time. When making connections, allow enough wire to make a neat run to each part as shown in Fig. 3-66. Allow about 2 ft of wire for connections between the mounting board and cabinet so the mounting board can be more easily

Fig. 3-64 Terminal markings on a three-way crossover.

Fig. 3-65 Quick-disconnect terminals.

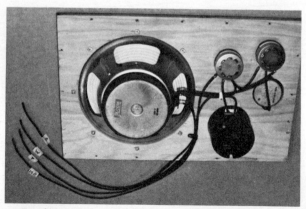

Fig. 3-66 Arrangement and identification of wires when the crossover is mounted inside the cabinet.

installed. If the crossover is in the cabinet, identify the wires which go to the crossover with small pieces of tape. Check the polarity of the terminal strip on the back of the cabinet and connect the crossover to the correct terminal posts. For reference, schematic diagrams of the crossover connections are shown in Fig. 3-67 for 6-dB- and 12-dB-per octave crossovers.

◈ **A WORD OF CAUTION:** To reduce burnout, some tweeters require a special protection circuit which has a capacitor and sometimes a small choke (wire coil). Be sure to check the directions supplied with the tweeters. If a protection circuit is required, be sure to use it to prevent tweeter burnout.

STEP 46.
L-Pad Connections.   The L-pad will allow you to control the loudness of the midrange or tweeter drivers. Better-quality speakers use two L-pads for control of both drivers. Figure 3-68 shows examples of the connections for one or two L-pads.

STEP 47.
Install Driver Mounting Board.   Place the cabinet on its back, but make sure the terminal strip connectors are not lying on any object which may apply pressure and cause breakage. Place the driver mounting board into its proper location on the cabinet. Install the mounting screws (painted black) by applying a little bar soap or wax to the threads. Hold the screwdriver firmly, as shown in Fig. 3-69, so it will not slip off the screw head and cause injury or damage. Drive the screws all the way in, but do not tighten them firmly until all screws are in place. Tighten screws evenly by going from one to another until they are equally tight.

Grille Covering

The grille of a speaker can be a regular inset, a full-front, or a sculptured foam. Each grille has different advantages and methods of installation. All grilles, however, help protect the drivers and add to the attractive appearance of the completed speakers.

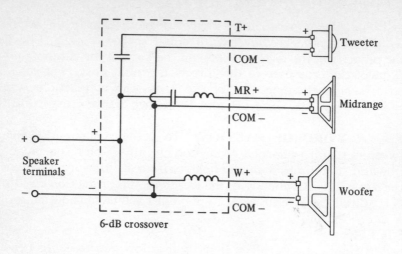

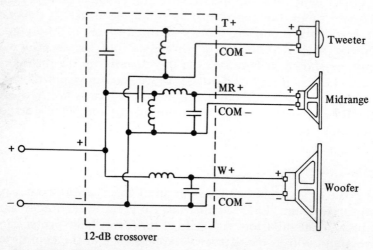

Fig. 3-67 Schematic diagrams of three-way crossover circuits.

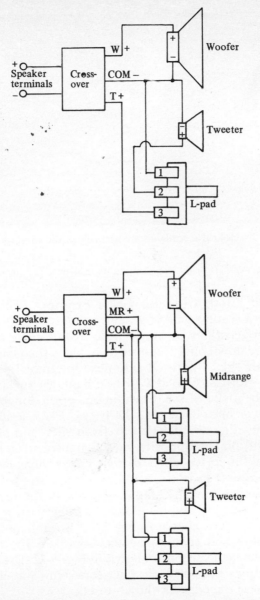

Fig. 3-68 Connections for using one or two L pads.

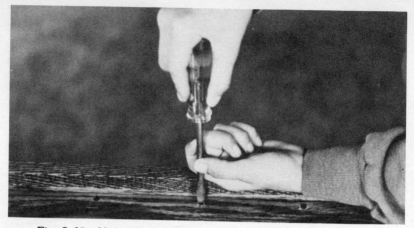

Fig. 3-69 Hold the screwdriver securely while driving screws.

STEP 48.

Install Grille Cloth (Regular Grille Frame). These instructions are for a regular grille frame. If you have a full-front grille, follow the suggestions in Step 49. To install grille cloth, place the cloth face down on a clean surface. Place the grille frame on cloth with the black-painted side next to cloth. Use a scissors to trim the cloth size so it will be about 1½ in larger on all sides than the grille frame. Start on one of the longer sides and pull cloth over onto back of grille frame. Place a staple in the center of one edge about half-way from each end as shown in Fig. 3-70. Pull on the opposite side to lightly stretch the cloth and apply a staple to center of that edge. Next, do the same procedure on each end.

After each edge has one staple, go back to the first side and install the remaining staples along the edge with a spacing of about 1½ in apart as shown in Fig. 3-71. Stretch and staple the remaining side and then the ends. Complete the corners by snipping open each corner as shown in Fig. 3-72. Use a hammer to set all staples firmly. With a scissors, trim the cloth which is hanging over the edge as shown in Fig. 3-73.

Fasten the loose cloth edges with masking tape. Start the tape at one corner and apply it all the way around the four edges as

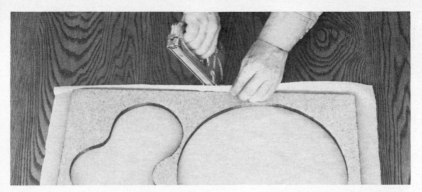

Fig. 3-70   Placement of the first staple to begin fastening grille cloth.

Fig. 3-71   Spacing staples on edge of grille frame.

Fig. 3-72   Snipping in the corner so the cloth can be folded to make a smooth corner.

Fig. 3-73 Trimming grille cloth.

shown in Fig. 3-74. Cut the tape at each corner and press it onto the cloth and grill back for a neat appearance as shown in Fig. 3-75.

STEP 49.
Install Grille Cloth (Full-Front Grille).   Grille cloth can be installed on full-front grilles in a way similar to a regular grille as was explained in Step 48. However, the staples are fastened to the back surface about ⅜ in in from the edge rather than on the edge surface. The grille cloth is trimmed about ¼ in beyond the staples. The corners must be pulled slightly tight to remove any wrinkles from the front side. Carefully fold the extra corner cloth onto the back and staple it in place. Apply 1 in wide masking tape to the cloth edge on the back side as shown in Fig. 3-76.

STEP 50.
Install Grille Frame Fasteners.   The grille frame is usually fastened to the cabinet with a hook-and-loop material. Only four small pieces of about ½ in by ¾ in each are needed on the smaller speakers. The larger speakers should have ¾ in by 1 in pieces. Full-front grilles should have 1 in by 1½ in pieces of hook-and-loop material.

Install the material by removing its adhesive backing or by applying mixed two-part five-minute epoxy glue to the back of the material. Place the pieces about 1 in in from the edges, as shown in Fig. 3-77. If the material tends to curl up, apply a

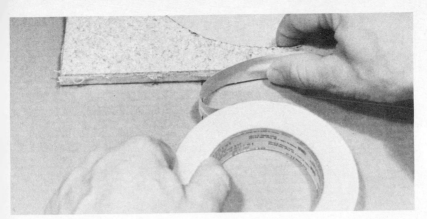

Fig. 3-74 Applying masking tape to the cloth edge of the grille frame.

Fig. 3-75 Professional appearance of taped cloth edge on the grille frame.

Fig. 3-76 Taping of the cloth on back side of a full-front grille frame.

STEP-BY-STEP BUILDING PROCEDURES   **161**

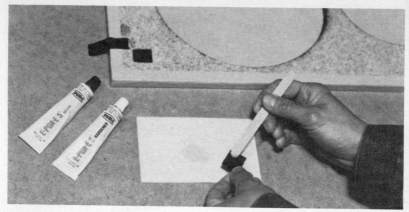

Fig. 3-77 Hook-and-loop material being glued with epoxy to the grille frame.

strip of masking tape over the material to hold it in place for a few minutes while the epoxy sets. Use all hook material on the grille frame and loop material on the driver mounting board. Also, near one of the corners, use five-minute epoxy glue and attach a small (about 3 in long by ½ in wide) piece of elastic fabric tape or twill tape to the back of the grille frame. Allow about 1¼ in of the tape to extend beyond the grille frame, as shown in Fig. 3-78. Either type of tape can be purchased at a fabric or sewing supply store. The elastic material is preferred because it will stretch and allow you to get a better hold for pulling when removing the grille frame.

Summary

Building of the speakers is now complete. However, if the speakers will be placed on a shelf or table, you may want to install a piece of felt material on the speaker bottoms to prevent scratches. Set the L-pad controls (if used) on the normal or central position. Install the grille, as shown in Fig. 3-79, and you are ready to begin testing and enjoying your new stereo speakers.

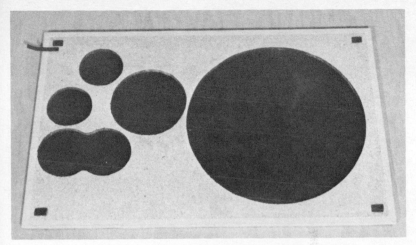

Fig. 3-78 Completed speaker grille with elastic tape applied to upper corner for pull tab to use when removing the grille from the speaker.

Fig. 3-79 Completed speaker with grille installed.

CHAPTER FOUR

Testing and Placing Your Speakers

After completing your speakers, a few simple tests can be made to check their performance. Most speaker projects work very well and only a few, if any, adjustments are needed. The polarity test will help determine if the speaker connections are correct. The L-pad test will allow you to hear the adjustments in the driver controls. If you have an audio signal generator, the frequency sweep test is useful in checking for any noises caused by loose boards or parts.

After testing your speakers, their placement in the listening room will be important to their performance. The sound of both low and high frequencies will be affected by the walls, the floor, the distance speakers are apart, and many other items.

4.1
Easy Speaker Tests

To begin the speaker tests, connect your speakers to the amplifier using No. 16 or No. 18 lamp (or similar) wire. The lamp wire will have two conductors. The insulation on one of these conductors will be labeled with small printing, a small rib, or other marking for identification. When a length of lamp wire is used, the wire marking is important for identifying each end of the same conductor.

Using the lamp wire, connect the speakers and amplifier in correct polarity. The positive (red or "+") amplifier terminal should be connected to the positive speaker terminal. The negative (black or "−") amplifier terminal should be connected to the negative speaker terminal.

If you have push-type terminals on the speakers or amplifier, as shown in Fig. 4-1, strip about ½ in of insulation off each wire and tin the wire by applying a light coat of solder to each bare end. If you have screw terminals on the speaker, you can use spade lugs, as shown in Fig. 4-2. To install spade lugs, remove about ¼ in of insulation from wire ends. Insert wire in the spade lug and solder or crimp in place.

When using bare wires under screw heads, strip about ½ in of insulation off each wire end. Wrap the strands tightly and tin the bare ends of the wire. Form the wire into a hook and

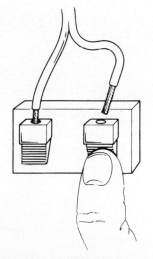

Fig. 4-1   Push-type terminals for speaker connections.

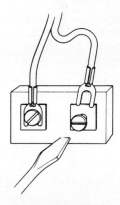

Fig. 4-2   Spade lugs and screw terminals.

wrap it around the screw head, as shown in Fig. 4-3. Note that wire which is *not* soldered and *not* wrapped correctly can cause a short between the terminals.

Now get ready for the most exciting part of the project, the "first listening test"! Select a recording you enjoy, start the music source, and slowly turn up the volume to a comfortable level. The sound should be pleasant and enjoyable.

Speaker Polarity

Good low-frequency sound depends on both speakers moving together at the same time. If all connections are correct, the speakers will have good bass sound; but if they are wrong, the bass sound will be noticeably weaker.

◆ **A WORD OF CAUTION:** The following test should *not* be used on the older tube-type amplifiers since disconnecting speaker wires during operation can cause serious amplifier damage.

To make the polarity test, use the following steps:

1. Place the speakers side-by-side and facing you at a distance of about 8 ft.

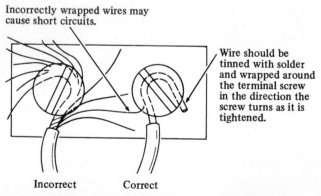

Fig. 4-3 **Examples of correct and incorrect speaker wire connections.**

2. Use a selection of music which has good bass sounds.
3. Set the amplifier for *mono* operation.
4. Turn the bass control to *max.*
5. Use a comfortable listening level of volume.
6. Listen closely to the music for a few (10) seconds and notice the amount of bass sound.
7. With the amplifier still playing, remove the speaker connections of just *one* speaker from the back of the amplifier. Now, hold wire ends on the terminals in a *reversed* order of polarity (the wire that was on the red terminal should now be on the black), as shown in Fig. 4-4.
8. Notice the loudness of the bass sound. Repeat the switching of connections a few times to recheck the sound.
9. The connections which give you the loudest bass sounds are the correct polarity.
10. If the speakers are placed face-to-face, you may notice this polarity difference even more.

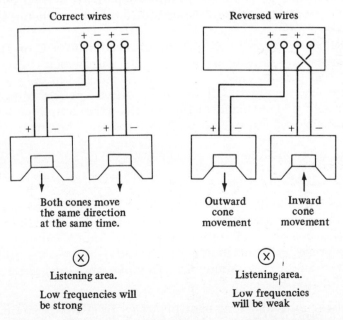

Fig. 4-4   Connection of wires for checking speaker polarity.

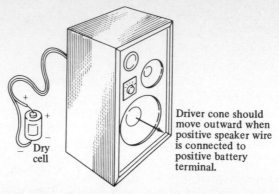

Driver cone should move outward when positive speaker wire is connected to positive battery terminal.

Dry cell

Fig. 4-5 A battery can be used to check speaker or driver polarity for correct stereo sound.

11. Fasten the wires to the amplifier terminals in their correct polarity. (Mark the wires for future reference when making connections.)

12. Speaker polarity can also be checked with a C or D cell battery, as shown in Fig. 4-5. The wire which causes the driver cone to move outward when touched to the positive battery terminal will be the positive speaker wire and should be connected to the positive (red) amplifier terminal. Check both stereo speakers for correct polarity.

L-Pad Check

A simple way to determine if the L-pad controls are working is the *white-noise* test. White noise is a name given to the noise you hear between FM stations when the "mute" button is *off*. White noise has short bursts of all audio frequencies and its sound resembles a hissing noise. To make the L-pad check, use the following steps:

1. Set the amplifier tone controls to *flat* or center position and switch *off* the filters and "loudness" control.

2. Switch *off* the "FM mute" control on the receiver.
3. Adjust the FM receiver for a location between FM stations and bring the volume up slowly.
4. Adjust the balance control so just one speaker produces sound.
5. Adjust the volume for a comfortable (not loud) listening level.
6. Adjust each L-pad and notice the change in sound. If you can hear the sound change as you adjust each L-pad, you will know each one is working to control the drivers. Leave the L-pads in a "normal" or "flat" setting, as shown in Fig. 4-6. You may later want to change this setting when listening to music to suit your personal listening taste.
7. Switch the balance control to the other channel and repeat this procedure for the other speaker.
8. When test is complete, turn volume down.

Frequency Sweep (Optional)

(This test can be performed if you have an audio signal generator or test record.) The sweep test of a speaker will help locate loose speaker parts and determine if the drivers and crossover are working properly. The audio signal generator (often available at service shops and school electronics labs) is used for a

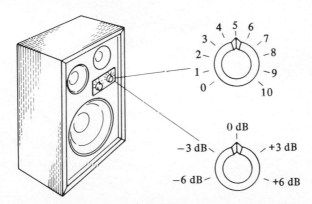

Fig. 4-6 Adjustment of L-pads for a normal, flat response.

frequency sweep test. In this test, the generator is swept (dialed) through all of the audio frequencies from 20 Hz to 20,000 Hz. A stereo test tone record can also be used to generate a frequency sweep. These records are often available from record supply stores.

◉ **A WORD OF CAUTION:** During this sweep test, keep the amplifier power very low (about 10 percent of the speaker power rating or less) to prevent damage to the drivers.

To make the frequency sweep test, use the following steps:

1. Connect an audio signal generator to the left "aux" input on the amplifier, as shown in Fig. 4-7.
2. Set the amplifier for *mono* operation.
3. Set the bass and treble tone controls for *flat* response.
4. Make sure the filters and "loudness" controls are *off.*
5. Adjust the balance control so only one speaker is operating.

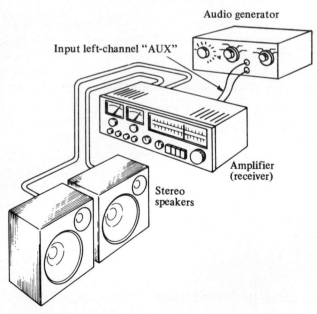

Fig. 4-7 Equipment connection for doing a frequency sweep test.

6. Set the audio generator for sine waves of 1000 Hz.
7. If the speaker has L-pad controls, adjust them for a center or normal setting.
8. Bring up the volume to a comfortable but not loud (about 80 dB at 3 ft) listening level. Once again, keep the amplifier volume low because speakers can be easily burned out with test tones.
9. Slowly adjust the generator for lower frequencies until you reach 20 Hz.
10. If you notice any buzzing or strange sounds, examine the speaker and determine their cause while the sound is being made.
11. After completing the low-frequency test, return to 1000 Hz.
12. Do *not* increase the volume on the amplifier during any of these tests. Adjust the audio frequency slowly upward to 20,000 Hz. Notice if the loudness is constant and smooth. Weak sounds in the frequency sweep may indicate that the crossover and drivers are not working properly or have exceeded their performance limits. Remember, your hearing may not be perfect, so a weak sound could be the fault of your hearing. The opinion of a second person may be helpful in determining speaker performance with a sweep test.
13. Return to 1000-Hz test tone and adjust the balance control so the sound will be produced from the other speaker. Repeat the frequency sweep checks.
14. When test is complete, turn volume control down and disconnect the audio signal generator.
15. After completing this test, you should have a better idea of the low- and high-frequency performance as well as location of any causes of noise. You will find, however, that during the playing of *music*, the low- and high-frequency response performance can be extended farther by using the tone controls and/or loudness control.

4.2
Placement of Speakers

The performance of every speaker is affected by its location in the listening room. Low-frequency sounds, for example, are affected by any object which reflects sound. High frequencies are more direct and are affected by the height and angle of the speakers. Finding the best location often requires some experimenting with speaker placement. The following suggestions and information in this section will help you find the location which works well for your speakers.

As you place your speakers for best sound, try to keep your system balanced. The two speakers should be at equal heights and equal distances from walls and floors. Finding the best location often requires rearranging some shelves or furniture and experimenting with the sound. The location you decide on will probably be a compromise between best sound and best furniture arrangement.

Height and Angle

The sound from the tweeter has a narrow dispersion pattern compared to a woofer. High frequencies, therefore, are strongest directly in front of the tweeter, as shown in Fig. 4-8. Placing the speakers so the tweeter is about ear level will give you the best high-frequency sound. If the speakers are large and on the floor, a small board or other object can be placed under the

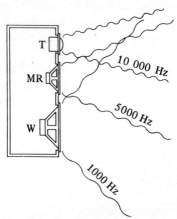

Fig. 4-8 Dispersion of sounds in relation to their frequency.

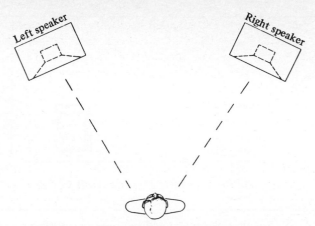

Fig. 4-9　An inward angle of speakers improves high-frequency performance.

front of the speaker to tilt it slightly back and improve the tweeter angle to the listener.

The speakers should also be turned slightly inward as shown in Fig. 4-9. Proper height, upward angle, and inward angle each help keep the tweeters pointed at the general listening area for best performance of high-frequency sounds.

Distance from Wall

Low-frequency sounds which many people enjoy often sound different (usually louder) as the speakers are moved near a wall or corner location. The sound changes because hard surfaces reflect low frequencies similar to the way a mirror reflects light. Of course, if the hard surfaces are covered by a soft material such as a rug or curtain, the reflections will be less. The four following examples, with brief descriptions, suggest areas to try when experimenting with speaker location.

No Nearby Surfaces.　When speakers are placed away from the walls on small supports as shown in Fig. 4-10, the sound

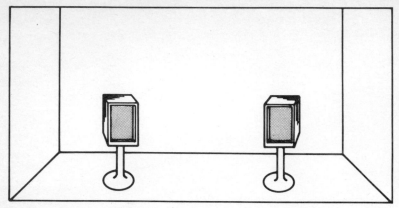

Fig. 4-10 Speaker placement with no reflecting surfaces nearby.

has *no* reflecting surfaces nearby. Most of the sound you hear from this location will be directly from the speakers. This location may work well if speakers have large woofers with very strong low-frequency response. Small speakers, however, will sound weak with this placement.

One Reflecting Wall (or Floor). When one hard surface is near the speakers as shown in Fig. 4-11, the low-frequency sound will be slightly stronger (3 dB) compared to no reflecting surfaces. This is equal to doubling the amplifier power. The hard surface can be either a wall or a floor. Try this placement if your speaker needs just slightly more bass sound.

Two Reflecting Surfaces. A noticeable increase in low-frequency loudness (6 dB) will be produced from two reflecting surfaces, as shown in Fig. 4-12. The surfaces can be either two walls, or a wall and a floor. The increase will be about equal to 4 times more amplifier power on the low bass sounds when compared to using no reflecting surfaces. This placement is very common for many stereo speakers.

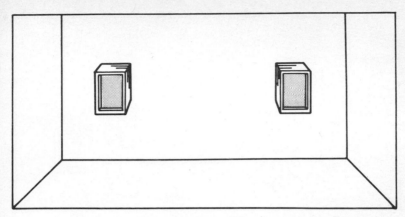

Fig. 4-11   Speaker placement with one nearby surface.

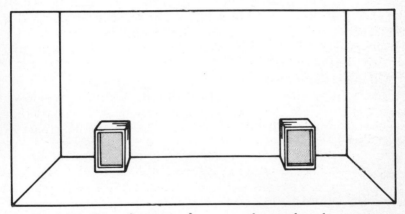

Fig. 4-12   Two reflecting surfaces near the speaker placement.

Three Reflecting Walls.   Corner placement between two walls and a floor (or ceiling), as shown in Fig. 4-13, will produce a large increase (9 dB) in the loudness of the low frequencies and make them seem almost twice as loud. This increase is about equal to 8 times more amplifier power when compared to a

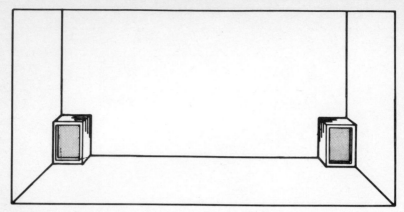

Fig. 4-13   Corner placement of speakers with three reflecting surfaces.

speaker with no nearby reflecting surfaces. A small bookshelf speaker may begin to sound like a big speaker by using this placement. This placement is usually not recommended for large speakers which may become boomy-sounding with this sort of location.

Although the idea of corner placement seems good for many speakers, it is often not practical due to furniture, windows, doors, shelves, etc. Also, the speakers may be so far apart that the stereo image will be lost as explained in the next part of this section.

Speaker Separation

The realism of the image created by stereo sound depends partly on the spacing of the two speakers. When the speakers are too close, the sound seems like it is from just one source. However, if the speakers are too far apart, the sound develops a "dead" spot in the center.

The correct distance between speakers is determined by the distance between the speakers and listening area. In general, speakers should be separated from each other by about as much as the distance between the speakers and the listener. However, a listener can move up to twice that distance away from

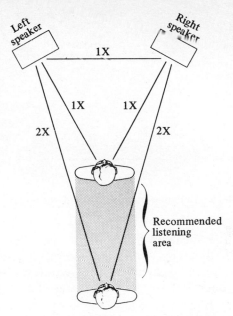

Fig. 4-14 Speaker separation and listening areas.

the speakers and still receive good stereo sound, as shown in Fig. 4-14. As an example: if the speakers are 8 ft apart, the listening area for good stereo sound will be from 8 to 16 ft from the speakers. Some listeners prefer more or less stereo separation. The best way to find the amount of separation you enjoy is to try a few different spacings starting with the suggested range.

Conditions to Avoid

Most stereo speakers will work well in the locations you choose, but there are some conditions which can cause poor performance, damage, or injury, and should be avoided. Here is a brief list of conditions to avoid in placing your speakers:

1. Do *not* set the speakers on metal shelves as the shelves will often rattle from loud sound.

Fig. 4-15   Enjoying your completed stereo speakers.

2. Do *not* set the speakers on the same shelf (or table) as turntable or "feedback howling" may be produced.
3. Do *not* set the speakers in front of windows as some of the sound will be lost through the glass and sunlight may fade the wood color.
4. Do *not* set speakers on weak or tippy shelves (or tables) as their weight may cause the supports to fall.
5. Do *not* run speaker wires across rugs or floors where people may catch them with their feet when walking and cause injury or damage.
6. Do *not* operate speakers at very loud levels if the sound seems distorted. This condition of high power can damage drivers.
7. Do *not* set loose items on top of speakers which may rattle during loud sounds.
8. Do *not* place anything in front of the speakers.

Conclusion

After testing and placing your new stereo speakers, they are ready for use. The enjoyment you and others receive when listening to favorite selections of music from your own hand-crafted speakers is a pleasant reward for your time and work, as shown in Fig. 4-15. When the speakers look attractive, the enjoyment is even greater.

Glossary

A-B Test A method of evaluating the relative performance of two or more components or systems by switching quickly from one to the other.

Acoustic Feedback Annoying interference created when vibrations from loudspeakers are picked up by the phono cartridge or microphone and then amplified by the sound system.

Acoustic Fiberglass A special glass-fiber material designed to damp the reflected sound inside a speaker cabinet.

Acoustic Suspension A speaker with a sealed speaker cabinet.

Acoustics The science of sound. Also, the sound character of halls and rooms.

Air Suspension An acoustic suspension speaker.

Alnico Magnet A magnet which is about twice as strong as a ceramic magnet and used to provide the magnetic field for the driver.

Aluminum Oxide Sandpaper A sandpaper coated with a very hard material which can be used to sand all types of hardwood.

Anechoic Chamber (Room) A specially designed room, used for testing microphones and speakers, rendered acoustically dead by sound-absorbing material.

Attenuation The reduction of an electrical signal.

Baffle A board used to direct sound movement inside a speaker cabinet.

Basket The metal frame of a driver.

Bass The audio frequency range between 20 and 1000 Hz.

Bass Reflex A type of speaker enclosure in which the speaker's rear wave emerges from an auxiliary opening, or port, to strengthen the bass (low) frequencies.

179

Battens Small boards used to fasten the front and back to the sides of a speaker cabinet.

Bobbin A paper or metal tube on which the voice coil is wrapped and connected to the driver cone.

Burnout A permanent condition caused by the voice coil of the driver becoming too hot, which results in total failure or distorted sound.

Ceramic Magnet A special magnetic compound pressed into a flat shape and used to provide the magnetic field for the driver.

Channels Two complete sound paths through the stereo equipment which represent the left and right sides of the performers.

Circuit Breakers A protection device used on amplifiers and some crossover circuits to prevent equipment damage from excessively high power.

Clipping A distorted sound condition where the speaker or amplifier is forced beyond its maximum output level.

Coaxial Driver A driver which has two or more voice coils and cones assembled on one frame for good frequency response.

Compliance The stiffness of the cone suspension. Very soft (easy to move) suspensions are called "high-compliance."

Cone The diaphragm of the driver which is moved by the voice coil and produces sound.

Continuous Power The amount of power each channel of an amplifier can deliver when fed with a continuous sine wave at a specified distortion level.

Crossover An electronic circuit (network) which passes the low-, mid-, and high-frequency music signals to the drivers (bass, midrange, or tweeter) which can most efficiently produce those sounds.

Crossover Frequency The frequency where the signals for a woofer and midrange driver, or a midrange and tweeter driver, meet with equal output levels which are usually 3 dB below the average output level.

Cutoff Frequency The frequency where the power of the signal has been reduced by one-half (3 dB).

Damping Reducing the movement of a driver cone by mechanical or electrical means after the music signal has changed or stopped.

Decibel (dB) A numerical expression of acoustical or electrical ratios, such as the relative strength of a sound or an electrical signal.

Dispersion The spreading of sound as it leaves the speaker.

Distortion Noises or changes in the sound which are not part of the original music.

Double-Line Layout Using two lines spaced about ⅛ in apart when marking boards so the saw cut can be made between the lines for accurate finished board sizes.

Driver A device for changing electrical signals to mechanical motion which becomes sound.

Ducted Port A type of bass-reflex speaker enclosure which uses a tube in the reflex port to tune the low-frequency sounds for improved performance.

Dust Cap A paper, cloth, or metal cap placed over the bobbin on the cone to prevent dust and dirt from entering the voice coil area.

Dynamic A driver which has a coil of wire that can move within a magnetic field area.

Dynamic Range The range of loudness, or sound intensity, that an audio component or instrument can reproduce without distortion.

EIA Electronic Industries Association.

Enclosure The speaker cabinet.

Fidelity The amount of trueness a reproduced sound has compared to the original sound, implying minimum distortion and a flat frequency response.

Finishing Nails Nails which have very small heads that can be driven slightly below the wood surface to improve cabinet appearance.

Flat Response Variations of less than 1 dB above or below an average response level.

Flatness The variations in a frequency response curve between its high-frequency and low-frequency cutoff points.

Frame The metal structure of the driver which holds the parts in correct alignment.

Free-Air Resonance The frequency a woofer driver can most efficiently produce when out of a cabinet.

Frequency The number of wave cycles which pass a particular point or occur in a circuit each second, measured in hertz (Hz).

Frequency Response The range of frequencies being produced by the audio equipment.

FTC Federal Trade Commission.

Full-Front Grille A grille which covers the entire front surface of the speaker.

Full-Range A driver which is designed to cover a wide range of sound.

Gap Area The small area around the voice coil where the magnetic field is concentrated and very strong.

Golden Ratio A ratio of depth, width, and height dimensions which is approximately 0.6 to 1 to 1.6 for designing a cabinet which has a pleasing appearance and sound.

Grille Cloth An open weave cloth used to cover the front of a speaker.

Half-Roll A soft polyfoam or butyl rubber suspension.

Hardwood Veneer Plywood A board made from several layers of wood with a thin layer of hardwood such as oak, walnut, or birch on each of the two outer surfaces.

Hertz A unit of frequency equal to one cycle per second. The name is in honor of Heinrich Hertz, an early electrical scientist.

Hi-Fi (High-Fidelity) A term which refers to very high quality sound performance from audio components.

Hook-and-Loop Material (Velcro) A special fabric with small plastic hooks on one part and small loops on the other part which can be used to hold the grille on the speaker cabinet.

Horn A speaker design using a funnel-shaped enclosure to couple the sound vibrations of a diaphragm or cone to the surrounding air.

Impedance A measurement of electrical resistance in a speaker.

Kiln A large oven for drying wood to prevent cracking or shrinkage after building.

Listening Fatigue A condition where the listener quickly becomes tired of the music because of small distortions in the sound.

Listening Taste The personal choice in sound loudness, frequency response, or other sound characteristics which a person enjoys.

Load The electrical or mechanical work to be done.

Loudness The volume (strength) of the sound.

L-pad A simple electric device with a control for adjusting the amount of music signal going to a driver.

Magnet Ceramic or Alnico material placed on the back of the driver frame.

Magnet Assembly The iron and magnet pieces that work together to concentrate the magnetic field in the voice coil area of the driver.

Midrange The audio frequency range between 1000 and 4000 Hz.

Mounting Flanges The outer edges of a driver frame which are used for mounting the driver to a speaker cabinet.

Music Power The highest power that will be used in any part of the music signal; may be twice as high as the average power used for the music.

Mylar Trademark for a plastic used for cones or domes in some midrange and tweeter drivers.

Natural Sound The sound as it was produced by the musical performer.

Noise Unnatural sounds in the music such as static, hissing, or buzzing.

Octave A multiple of a reference frequency. For example, the first octave up from a 2000 Hz signal is 4000 Hz, and the first octave down is 1000 Hz.

Ohm A unit of electrical resistance.

Overload To feed into a system a signal that exceeds the capability of the system; results in distortion.

Particle Board Small chunks of wood ground, pressed, and glued into a flat board shape.

Passive Radiator A speaker that uses two woofer drivers. The first woofer is powered by the amplifier, while the other woofer (the drone) operates from the air pressure produced inside the cabinet by the first woofer. Efficiency at low frequencies is improved by this method.

Peak The maximum voltage or power level of a signal.

Peak Power An older power rating now seldom used in audio work. It refers to electrical power measured without the standard rms correction factor.

Penny (d) A measurement of nail size and length.

Phase A term which describes the relative position of one sound wave with respect to another. Two identical waves are in-phase when crests meet crests and troughs meet troughs, which allows the strength of the two waves to be added together. Two identical waves are out-of-phase when the crests of one wave meet the troughs of another, which causes the signal to become weaker because one wave cancels the other.

Phase Distortion (Shift) A change in the natural timing sequency between the wave patterns of two signals so the crests of the two waves do not occur at the same time and place.

Piezoelectric A special metallic crystal which will quickly bend when an electrical signal is applied.

Pitch The frequency of a musical tone.

Polarity The positive and negative driver, crossover, and amplifier terminals.

Poles (Magnetic) The regions of a magnet which produce the (invisible) magnetic lines of force.

Ported Reflex A speaker cabinet which has an opening (port) to improve efficiency at low frequencies.

Resonance The tendency of a mechanical or electric device to vibrate or oscillate at a particular frequency.

rms Root mean square; a commonly accepted standard of electrical voltage or power measurements.

rms Power The standard and accepted method of measuring amplifier power per channel; required by the Federal Trade Commission to be at 1000 Hz into 8-ohm speakers with less than 1 percent distortion.

Rosin-Core Solder A special solder used for electronic work.

Sensitivity A rating to determine how much sound will be produced from a speaker when using a signal of standard power (1 W) and frequency.

Sine Wave A smooth S-shaped wave when viewed on an oscilloscope or graph, consisting of a single-frequency signal.

Sound Level The strength of sound (volume) being produced.

Speaker Efficiency The ratio of electrical power needed to produce a sound to the measured sound power which results.

Speaker Power The amount of sound a speaker will produce; depends on efficiency and electrical power in watts.

Spider A flexible part of the driver which holds the voice coil in proper alignment with the magnet assembly.

Square Wave A special square-shaped wave which can be used for testing electronic circuit performance.

Squawker A term sometimes used to refer to the midrange driver in a multiple-driver speaker.

Standing Waves Audio waves occurring in a confined area and resulting in small areas of strong and weak sound levels, which are not directly related to the distance from the source.

Surround The outer suspension of a driver cone.

Suspension (Surround) The area around the cone which holds the cone in correct alignment during its movement.

Tack Cloth A soft cloth which is damp and slightly sticky for removing dust from a cabinet surface before applying a finish coat.

Terminal Strip Connections installed on the back of a speaker for the wires which run to the amplifier.

Three-Way A speaker system which has a woofer, midrange, and tweeter driver for good performance over the full audio frequency range.

Tinning A process of coating wires or the soldering iron tip with a thin layer of solder.

Tone Control A preamplifier control circuit used to boost or reduce the bass and treble sounds to suit the listener's choice.

Transient A distortion of sound caused by a slight delay in response of an amplifier or speaker to a quick change in a music signal.

Treble The high end of the audio frequency range, which typically includes the frequencies from 4000 to 20,000 Hz.

Tweeters The smallest drivers in a speaker which are used to produce the high-frequency sounds.

Vent An opening or port in a speaker enclosure which is sometimes used to improve low-frequency performance.

Voice Coil Many turns of small diameter wire wrapped in a coil, connected to the driver cone, and terminated in two terminals on the back of the driver frame.

Weather Stripping A soft foam material used to seal the edges of doors and windows, and used in speaker construction to seal the front of the cabinet to the batten boards.

White Noise A type of noise (such as found between FM stations) which contains an equal number of all audio frequencies.

Whizzer A small cone attached to the front of a larger driver cone for producing better high-frequency response.

Woofer The large driver used for producing the bass sounds.

Index

556